Foreign Languages
and Education
in Western Europe

Other Works by W. D. Halls

Maurice Maeterlinck: A Study of his Life and Thought (Oxford University Press, 1960).

Society, Schools, and Progress in France (Pergamon Press, 1965).

Translations of:

HUBERT AND MAUSS: *Sacrifice: its Nature and Function* (Cohen and West, 1964).

CAPELLE, JEAN: *Tomorrow's Education: The French Experience* (Pergamon Press, 1967).

FÜHR, CHRISTOPH: *Educational Reform in Germany* (UNESCO Institute for Education, Hamburg, 1970)

Foreign Languages
and Education
in Western Europe

by

W. D. HALLS

GEORGE G. HARRAP & CO. LTD
London   Toronto   Wellington   Sydney

First published in Great Britain 1970
by GEORGE G. HARRAP & CO. LTD
182–184 High Holborn, London, W.C.1

© *W. D. Halls* 1970

ISBN 0 245 50463 X

C

*Composed in Monotype Times and printed
at the Pitman Press, Bath
Made in Great Britain*

Preface

This study reviews some important aspects of modern-language teaching in the schools of Western Europe. It first deals with the significance of languages in the European context, and shows how trends in policy have emerged from the political and educational decisions taken in the various countries. Secondly, it assesses the progress made towards European agreement on the aims and objectives of language teaching. Next it sketches how the new discipline of applied linguistics over the past decade has influenced the re-thinking of teaching methods. The key facet of learning a foreign language—how the pupil learns about the foreign culture and civilization—is discussed. It then deals with some of the problems encountered in the teaching and learning situation and the solutions propounded. Lastly it raises the question of how linguistic competence is assessed and how evaluation might be improved. It is these topics that are at present the principal subjects in the discussion of modern-language teaching in Western Europe.

The main emphasis in that discussion, and consequently in this book, is on the role that foreign languages play in secondary education. This is not to decry the significant pioneer work that is going on in teaching younger children, but such work is not yet sufficiently widespread. On the other hand, over the past generation, secondary education has become recognized as the right of all. It is likewise generally accepted that at least one foreign language should form part of the curriculum for all pupils at this stage. It is above all this fact that has contributed to the revolution in language teaching in a significant way. Moreover, the extension of language teaching to the less gifted children has affected the teaching of the intellectual élites. In the academic secondary school, in those countries where it survives, an intense debate as to the content, method, and evaluation of language courses is proceeding.

The European Ministers of Education, whose representatives met under the auspices of the Council of Europe in May 1969 in London, have adopted a resolution which aims at converting into reality the

5

slogan "a modern language for everybody by 1980". Thus the goal for the 1970s is achievement of a measure of bilingualism in Western Europe. This has therefore become a commitment for everyone— teacher, parent, and pupil, no less than the man in the street.

This monograph, which it is hoped may interest not only the languages specialist and the educational administrator, but also the informed layman, is consequently a report of work in progress. At the same time it strives to indicate the consequences of policies, to highlight deficiencies, and to consider remedies. It is based in part upon an inquiry conducted within the framework of the Oxford/ Council of Europe Study for the Evaluation of the Curriculum and Examinations (OCESECE Study), a survey of modern-language teaching within the member countries of the Council of Europe, with the assistance of that body. I am particularly grateful for the support and help of two of its senior officials—M. Bemtgen and Mr Sven Nord. The Gulbenkian Foundation also kindly provided financial support. I should also like to thank Mr Peter Figueroa, my research associate. None of these organizations or persons, however, bears any responsibility for this book: any inaccuracies, no less than the glosses put upon the information gathered, are entirely my own.

W. D. H.

Department of Educational Studies,
Oxford University
December 1969

Contents

Tables

COUNTRY ABBREVIATIONS USED IN TABLES

Au	Austria
Bg	Belgium
Cy	Cyprus
Dk	Denmark
Ge	Federal Republic of Germany (1)
Fi	Finland
Fr	France
Ic	Iceland
Ir	Republic of Ireland
It	Italy
Lux	Luxembourg
Ma	Malta
Neth	Netherlands
No	Norway
Sp	Spain
Sd	Sweden
Sw	Switzerland
Tu	Turkey
UK	United Kingdom (2)

(1) With very few exceptions all information given is characteristic of the *Land* of Hessen and, except where otherwise stated, refers to the situation in January 1969. Where the information refers to the whole of the Federal Republic this is apparent from the context.

(2) In tables and diagrams the abbreviation UK (E) means that the information given refers only to England and Wales. In the text care has been taken to distinguish between the use of "Britain", "England", etc.

Chapter 1

The Significance of Languages in Western Europe

The political future of Western Europe has been variously characterized as being 'evolutionary', 'Atlanticized', 'a partnership', 'independent and federal', 'functional', or as remaining a 'Europe of nation states'. But no matter what governmental model may eventually be adopted in the 1970s, the means of communication between its constituent elements will become of increasing importance. After centuries of intolerable bloodshed and strife it may at last become clear that neither nationality nor race, religion nor political ideology, should prove insurmountable obstacles to this limited form of international understanding. But the barrier of language will still remain—a formidable one because it sets limits on the dimensions of our thought, colours our concept of civilization, and deeply affects the quality of our lives. Today cultural interpenetration is only possible through the medium of a multitude of tongues. The force for European unity represented by Latin when it was still the common mode of discourse among intellectuals has been dissipated. It is therefore vital to decide what languages should be taught in Western Europe, and what means for teaching them are available.

More particularly, criteria must be established for selecting the foreign languages to be taught in schools. A rough indicator of the 'importance' of any language is the number of people who use it as their natural means of communication. Several languages spoken in Western Europe rate highly on this criterion. Although Mandarin Chinese has at least double the number of native speakers, English comes second on the list, followed respectively by Spanish, Russian, and German. Within the top ten per cent of the world's languages, when measured by the same standard, also fall, in order, Portuguese, French, and Italian. Thus, of these eight languages, all save Chinese and Russian originated in Western Europe. Moreover, if one adds to the number of native speakers those who use certain languages as an alternative means of communication it is probable that a rank order of importance would then be: Chinese, English, Russian, French, Spanish, and German. By the cogent criterion of 'use', European languages—and particularly those of Western Europe—are plainly educationally indispensable.

On the European, as well as on the world scene, English and French enjoy a privileged position. Some 300 million people speak English as their mother tongue. Many others use it as their international means of communication: within Europe the Turk will communicate with the Swede in English; outside Europe the Nigerian will use it to communicate with the Indian. The polarization of world political power into American and Soviet hands has also stimulated the use of English as a second language. Outside North America, Britain, Ireland, and Australasia, there are vast tracts of Asia—notably the Indian sub-continent—and Africa where English is the *lingua franca;* it is also often the language of education, and likely to remain so until universal literacy in the indigenous languages has been achieved and textbooks have been written in them in sufficient number and at a sufficiently high level. Likewise, the French 'linguistic area' is almost as vast. Within Europe the Spaniard will probably use it to communicate with the Italian. Moreover, it would appear that *L'Afrique francophone* is on the way to achieving its own cultural identity. Nor must one forget that Montreal is the second largest French-speaking city in the world. There are, however, indications that in the schools of Europe the world-wide ramifications of English and French are comparatively neglected, and there is undue concentration upon Britain and France as the linguistic focus of interest.

Whereas Spanish, like English, derives much of its importance because of its widespread currency on the American continent, the case for German is almost entirely based on its use within Europe, despite the massive German migrations to the American mid-West. Although the claims of German have been muted up to now for political reasons, they must not be forgotten. There are, for example, few educated Central Europeans who do not know at least a smattering of the official language of the successive German or Austrian hegemonies under which their countries were once ruled.

Likewise, the importance of Russian must not be forgotten, although this is in part another case of political prejudice having impeded its spread in the schools of Western Europe.

In Western Europe English is the first foreign language most commonly taught. Spain is an exception: French, for historical, geographical, and cultural reasons has primacy. Two other exceptions are Belgium and Luxembourg, both of which have special linguistic problems. In Belgium until recently, for the French-speaking Walloons, Dutch (*Nederlands*) was the second national or first non-mother tongue language, as French was for the Flemings. In Luxembourg German is the medium of instruction in the lower grades of schooling, and French in the upper grades. Both these languages are technically 'foreign' ones, but are used as vehicular languages of instruction in place of Luxembourgeois. In West Germany certain districts of Baden-Württemberg also have French as their first foreign language, and various post-war cultural agreements between France and the Federal Republic have promoted measures to increase the number of pupils studying the respective languages. In Finland Swedish is a minority second national language. But elsewhere French is the usual second foreign language. In Britain it is, of course, the first foreign language largely because of historical ties, geographical proximity, and the world importance of the language. In some courses of secondary schooling the Netherlands stipulates the learning of three foreign languages, and Sweden at least two. In France a recent ruling has made the learning of a second foreign language optional. In England some Oxford and certain other university faculties stipulate that candidates for admission must have entrance qualifications in two foreign languages. France probably offers the greatest choice of foreign languages to its pupils—eight in all, including Arabic and Chinese. In Western Europe only France and Britain offer courses in Chinese. Countries usually allow minority languages to be studied, where they exist: in Britain, Welsh; in France, Basque and Breton; in Austria, Croatian, Slovene, and Hungarian.(1)

Some indication of the comparative 'spread' or diversification in languages taught can be gleaned from a study of England, France, and Germany. In England, for reasons already mentioned, French has always had primacy. The decision, taken perhaps before its consequences for policy were fully realized, to introduce French almost exclusively into the primary schools, and consequently into the non-academic secondary schools, has ensured the supremacy of that language until at least the next millennium. At the academic secondary level this pre-eminence is already well established. In fact, during the five-year period from 1962 to 1966, despite numerous semi-official attempts particularly to promote the learning of Russian, the relative proportions of candidates sitting for A Level in the General Certificate of Education examination in the various languages studied in English secondary schools has hardly varied. In 1965–66 (winter and summer examinations) the percentages of candidates were as follows:

**Table 1—England and Wales: The relative proportion of G.C.E.
A Level candidates in various languages, 1965–66**

Language	Percentage of total no. of language candidates
French	68·0
German	19·3
Spanish	6·3
Italian	1·6
Russian	1·6
Other	1·2
Total	± 100·0

Nor is this pattern peculiar to England. Comparable percentages of the numbers of pupils studying various languages in the three years of the terminal *lycée* course—equivalent in many respects to an English sixth-form college—were, in 1966:

**Table 2—France: The relative proportion of pupils studying
various languages in the *lycée***

Language	Percentage
English	58·8
German	19·6
Spanish	15·5
Italian	5·2
Russian	0·9
Other	trace
Total	± 100·0

The situation is almost the same in West Germany: in the *Gymnasium*, the comparable school, the percentages of pupils in 1966–67 studying the various languages were as follows:

**Table 3—Germany: The relative proportion of pupils studying
various languages in the *Gymnasium* (Hessen figures)**

Language	Percentage
English	67·3
French	31·6
Russian	0·5
Other	0·3
Total	± 100·0

The comparative pattern of language teaching that emerges is therefore as follows:(2)

Table 4—The comparative pattern of language teaching in England, France, and Germany

(rounded percentages)

	England	France	Germany
First modern language	68 (Fr)	59 (Eng)	67 (Eng)
Second modern language	19 (Ge)	20 (Ge)	32 (Fr)
Third modern language	6 (Sp)	16 (Sp)	1 (Ru)
Other modern languages	7 (It, Ru)	6 (It, Ru)	Trace (Sp, It)
Total	± 100	± 100	± 100

Such figures seem to be as the result of mere chance rather than as flowing from deliberate acts of educational policy by the various governments concerned. In Western Europe it is clear that English was promoted by the presence of American and British troops in the liberated or the occupied countries. Political judgments also enter, consciously or unconsciously, into educational decisions. In France, as has been mentioned already, the promotion of the study of German has been linked with the fostering of Franco-German understanding. Prejudice has undoubtedly entered into the reluctance of German schools to promote Russian. Whereas in East Germany it is the first foreign language, in West Germany it is usually the third foreign language. Save for West Berlin, it is taught only in the *Gymnasium*, the academic secondary school. In West Germany proper it is most widespread in North Rhine-Westphalia. Whereas in 1961, 6595 pupils in the Federal Republic were learning the language, the number dropped to 6289 after the building of the Berlin Wall and the consequent decrease in the number of refugees from the German Democratic Republic. By May 1967 the numbers had again risen to 7908, but even so this represented only 8 in 1000 *Gymnasium* pupils.(3) But if such reasons are explicable in the German context, the comparative neglect of Russian in English and French schools is not. It is surely no more difficult a language than Latin, which was the daily diet of the English grammar school pupil at least until the Second World War. Perhaps more important than all else, however, may be the lack of teachers in the less popular languages. This tends to be a self-perpetuating problem: pupils who learn certain languages at school tend to study the same languages in higher education, become teachers and teach them.

An even more serious problem for those who wish for the political or cultural integration of Western Europe is that the nations are producing comparatively few linguists versed in languages of Western Europe other than the three main ones, two of which, English and French, have undoubted world status. It is surprising that so little Italian is studied in Germany, whose greatest writer, Goethe, could write of Rome that he counted the day upon which he first entered that city as "a true rebirth".(4) Progress in learning what might be termed the 'minority' languages may in fact be impeded by the fashionable insistence that all languages should be learnt for oral communication. Yet, although it is clearly desirable that speaking skill should also be fostered in languages of less international currency, it is imperative that a reading knowledge at least should be taught to some pupils. In every European country for political, cultural, and economic reasons it is surely important that a well-educated minority should be able to appreciate, through the printed word and without translation, not only the glory of the Italian Renaissance, but, more mundanely, present-day social conditions in Flanders or the season's prospects for the Norwegian whaling fleet. Some efforts to impart reading skills in these less widely used languages are in fact made in West Germany in voluntary study groups (*Arbeitsgemeinschaften*) and in English sixth-forms in 'minority time' (school time used for subjects not taken in the leaving examination). But research as to how such reading skills can most rapidly be developed is urgently required.

It is clear that a European strategy for the choice of languages to be studied has yet to be worked out. If bilingualism is a desirable goal for everybody, then it is obvious that those who might be termed the future 'power élites' should at least be in some degree trilingual.

The lack of coherent linguistic policies by countries has already been noted. Perhaps Sweden is one country where, in a significant sector of its educational system—the upper academic secondary level —an attempt has been made to plan rationally for the languages to be taught. In the past there have been many qualitative estimates made as to the 'value' of the modern languages studied by the academically gifted. But the study undertaken by Urban Dahllöf,(5) made in connection with the reform of the pattern of the curriculum, is the most authoritative, because it also attempted to quantify the 'demand' for modern languages. It consisted of a survey made among those who might be termed the 'consumers' of upper academic secondary education (which in Sweden takes place in the *gymnasiet*). It was, incidentally, not confined to languages, but included all aspects of the secondary curriculum. Conducted on the same lines as a study in market research, the survey attempted to quantify the degree to which competence in foreign languages was valued by those who received the 'products' of the *gymnasiet*—*i.e.*, university teachers and leaders in public administration, trade, and industry. The results are reported here not only because of their intrinsic interest, but also because they could serve as a model to other countries as to how to proceed.

A questionnaire was circulated asking for ratings among these interest groups of the need each experienced for those studying foreign languages to be competent in different aspects of them. These aspects were defined as: reading comprehension; the ability to follow lectures in the foreign language; the ability to converse; to conduct correspondence with the help partially of a grammar and a diction-ary; to write letters or simple reports without such help; to write reports of a more complicated nature; to speak with good pronuncia-tion and intonation. At the same time the respondents were asked to rate how satisfactory they deemed to be the graduates from the *gymnasiet* they were receiving at the time.

The results of the survey showed that professors of the humanities, sciences, medicine, and technology all underlined the necessity for reading comprehension, the ability to understand lectures in the foreign language, and the ability to converse. For English, as com-pared with German and French, the degrees of competence required were much higher. The most exacting demands in foreign languages at university level were, of course, made by those professors who claimed the languages to be academic disciplines.

For public administration, trade, and industry, the results of the survey showed that the demands were just as exacting. All aspects of language skills were required to a high degree, particular emphasis being put on the ability to write letters with some help from a grammar and dictionary. The language most required was again English.

A detailed breakdown by university subjects showed that professors in all university subjects, save for a small minority, considered that English was essential for their students. German was considered essential by all professors in the following disciplines: geography, chemistry, history, economic history, history of literature, Scandi-navian languages, and Slavonic languages. French was considered essential by all professors of history, Spanish, and Slavonic languages. Among other languages Russian also occupied a significant place. In industry, particularly in banking and insurance, there was a need for Spanish, as well as the three main foreign languages.

The study in fact confirmed that foreign languages needed to be greatly emphasized in the curriculum of the new *gymnasiet*. More attention should be made to French than hitherto, and Russian and Spanish should also be offered. These recommendations have in fact

2

been largely implemented in the new curriculum, so that languages occupy an important place in all six sections of the *gymnasiet* (liberal arts, social sciences, economics, natural sciences, and technology).

Since English holds such a paramount place in Western Europe one important point of policy requires a decision, perhaps on the international plane: what *kind* of English should be taught? The English themselves do not appear to be chauvinistic on this point. One writer (6), for example, advocates "a neutral form of English, a language as free from national bias as Esperanto". At present the Continental pupil cannot but be bewildered by the many varieties of English that exist: Standard Southern English (Received Pronunciation), Northern English, Welsh English, Scottish English—and these within Britain itself. Even within the confines of Europe there is not only Standard British English, but also Standard Irish English. Beyond, there are, of course, other 'brands': Standard American English (that spoken by the educated American of the mid-West or the Eastern seaboard), with its sub-patterns of Canadian English and Southern American English, Standard Australasian English, and many other varieties which at present lack precise definition, but which must include some types of African English. For the teacher, as for the pupil, the criterion for all such variations must surely be that of comprehensibility. Those whose speech falls just within the 'limits' of comprehensibility must be capable of communicating mutually with each other and freely with all others well within those 'limits'. All such variations the pupil must be able to understand. But what speech must be given him as a model? What sometimes occurs at the moment in European classrooms is the teaching of what might be termed 'mid-Atlantic English', which is perhaps an even more depraved form of language than Étiemble's 'franglais'. On the other hand, if a neutral 'instrumental' form of English speech is to be the rule in European schools—and we must note that such a form has yet to be elaborated—or if American English is to prevail, then some cultural sacrifices will surely have to be made. Britain is part of Europe, and its culture is European, and it may be that this should be the determining factor. Although American authors are increasingly studied in some European countries, there can be little doubt that Britain and Ireland still share a richer literary and cultural patrimony than their transatlantic partners. Furthermore, the British Isles are more accessible to learners of English. These would seem to constitute cogent reasons for the retention of British English as the model in Western Europe, or for a new model of 'neutral English' to be worked out. To accept the 'British' option does not preclude the study, for example, of John Greenleaf Whittier or Oliver Wendell Holmes; to accept the 'neutral' option likewise does not rule out the reading of Shakespeare or Shaw. But the time has come for a deliberate policy decision to be made in which emphasis is placed on one form of English rather than another, and this must be consistently implemented for matters of pronunciation, lexis, content, or even orthography. Moreover, until some supra-national authority is set up to legislate on what is acceptable as English, at some stage of learning the language the pupil must be alerted as to the principal differences between North American and British usage. This may perhaps be done by a judicious comparison of selected entries in the *Oxford Dictionary* and *Webster's New Standard Dictionary*. In any case, it must be said that the present writer regards this choice between these two main forms of English as of limited duration. In the long run, but perhaps not even in the lifetime of our grandchildren, North American English, provided there is no unexpected reversal of trends, must eventually prevail.

For the other main European languages taught no such problems exist on a similar scale. With few exceptions France's former overseas possessions have not developed their own varieties of French to the same degree. In Canada the province of Quebec is now striving to rid itself of many local peculiarities—particularly the rather ugly *joual* pronunciation—and align itself linguistically more with Paris. For German, as long as seventy million Germans continue to occupy the heartland of Europe *Hochdeutsch* will continue, as in the past, to be the accepted form of the language taught in European schools.

That the most striking feature of European education over the past decade has been the extension of modern-language teaching to a larger number of pupils there can be little doubt. A renewal of the impetus for language learning had come first immediately after the end of the Second World War. By the late 1950s this force had almost been dissipated. At the same time the study of the classics had begun a steady decline in schools, with the result that nowadays many countries defer the introduction of Latin until pupils are about fourteen, and even fail to include Greek at all. The motivation for learning a foreign language increased with the spread of prosperity in Europe. With closer physical links, engendered by travel and tourism, technology, commerce and industry, radio and television, the necessity to communicate was heightened. In some countries, notably Sweden, the egalitarian view began to find currency that all children had the right to learn a modern language. Even in Germany, whose education system has up to now remained rigidly traditionalist, the increase in the numbers learning English has been phenomenal. The *Hauptschule* is the non-selective school for those who do not qualify for the *Realschule* (a semi-academic intermediate school) and the *Gymnasium* (the academic secondary school). Whereas in 1961 only 13·1 per cent of pupils in the *Haupt-schule* were learning English, by 1966 this figure had risen to 36·2 per cent—and 1·2 per cent were also learning French. At the lowest grades of the *Hauptschule*, where teachers are more readily available, over half are already learning English. The coverage is patchy, because teachers are few in rural areas, and also because some *Länder* are not yet convinced that all pupils are capable of learning English, so that only those who have obtained a creditable standard in other subjects are allowed to study it.

In the selective secondary schools there is almost 100 per cent coverage. In the *Realschule* in 1966, 99·3 per cent of pupils were studying English, and 26·8 per cent of pupils were also studying French. At the *Gymnasium* at least one foreign language is compulsory throughout the nine years of the course. In the seventh grade a pupil may begin a second foreign language, and in the ninth grade a third in some cases. English is again the predominant foreign language, with 87·8 per cent of pupils learning it at some stage of their course. Referring to English, moreover, one authoritative source optimistically asserts that "in the not far distant future the German nation may well have become, to some extent, a bilingual nation."(7) (From 1969 onwards all German children have been learning a foreign language.) There are other European nations also of which this might be said.

This second, post-war upsurge of enthusiasm on a European scale may perhaps be traced as far back as a conference of the Council of Europe held at Sèvres in 1959, when the work done by Professor Gougenheim and his collaborators on *Le Français Fondamental* became known to a wider European public. Later meetings at ministerial level passed resolutions intensifying language teaching at all grades of education. The European Ministers of Education stipulated that the programme should include the opening of national documentation and information centres on modern-language teaching; the extension by all European countries to pupils aged ten and over of the teaching of a widely spoken European language; the extension of language teaching later to pupils below that age; the modernization of teaching programmes; the expansion of study visits abroad and of exchanges; and the development of teacher-training programmes which would include courses on recent methodological findings, linguistics, and the use of educational technology.

As a result, in secondary education some countries have achieved almost 100 per cent foreign language coverage of the school population. This is the case for Austria, Cyprus, Luxembourg, the Netherlands, Sweden, West Berlin, and certain other regions in West

Germany. In the United Kingdom at present only some 60–65 per cent of secondary pupils are learning a foreign language, but this proportion increases yearly.

Furthermore, the extension of modern-language teaching into the elementary school continues. Here progress has been dramatic in Western Europe. The experiments carried out in French- and English-speaking Africa and India, in the United States and Soviet Russia, and in duo-lingual countries such as Belgium and Wales had demonstrated the desirability of language learning from an early age. Pilot projects had been carried out in the Paris region from 1956 onwards, in Stockholm from 1957, in Kassel from 1960, and in Leeds from 1961. In 1963 a massive pilot scheme for the introduction of French—and, in a few cases, German—into a large number of English primary schools was launched with the approval of the Department of Education and Science. Such a scheme has gathered impetus, so that although the final evaluation of what was originally a pilot scheme has not yet been made, it is certain there can be no turning back, and it is only a matter of time before the teaching of French in primary schools is generalized all over the United Kingdom.

These sweeping innovations were not made without difficulty. The outstanding problem has been the shortage of qualified teachers: it has been estimated that in order to introduce French into English primary schools over 60,000 trained teachers are required. By the mid-1960s the inefficiency of conventional language teaching methods was fairly generally accepted: the amount of time spent in acquiring even a modest competence in the language was out of all proportion. In 1966 M. Fourquet, a professor of German at the Sorbonne, declared that 45 per cent of his students had failed their university course because of phonetical and grammatical errors that should have been eliminated by the age of thirteen. A French inspector-general, M. Evrard, went further and asserted that the candidates he dealt with for teaching-posts in modern languages in secondary schools "are incapable of respecting elementary grammatical correctness in their translations into the target language. Yet these are students who have completed several years of specialized study and who have spent at least one or two years abroad."(8) Such complaints were by no means confined to France.

Meanwhile, however, a new generation was being brought up on different methods. In England the Nuffield Foundation and, later, the Schools Council had taken up the task of devising language-teaching materials for children in the 8–13 age range, and are at present engaged in producing further material in French, Spanish, Russian, and German for pupils aged 13–16. For French the materials devised have drawn heavily upon the pioneer research done by CREDIF in France. The advances made in applied linguistics and in educational technology had made innovations that had been advocated in a non-systematic way, and without the technical means for their realization, for over half a century. Today the language teacher is presented with an embarrassment of choice. Experience quickly showed that teaching materials devised for use in the native country were not suitable for wholesale adoption by other countries teaching a language at school level. The result has been a flood of audio-visual or audio-lingual aids of all kinds. In fact, the language laboratory and other ancillary aids have been brought into use before a proper rationale for their exploitation has really been evolved. But such problems are usual whenever educational progress is sought.

In terms of policy the very vitality of the movement towards the extension and reform of language teaching has had a liberalizing effect. In England, for example, the generalization of languages in secondary education has led to oblique and beneficial intervention both by the Department of Education and Science and local education authorities. Such intervention may ultimately have some indirect effect on the English examining boards, whose autonomy has been highly prized. They have undoubtedly ensured that an élite has reached high standards in certain aspects of language learning relevant to higher education, but more often than not they have acted as a brake upon new developments. In any case, the more centralized systems prevailing on the Continent are not so autocratic or bureaucratic as they might appear at first sight. As one German writer has put it, in respect of the directives issued centrally for the learning of English, these are "not concocted by some unnamed official in the Ministry but . . . formulated after ample discussion in committees of teachers and teachers' organizations."(9) Moreover, and this requires to be mentioned, unlike many of those who sit on the foreign-language panels of English examining boards and whose teaching experience has been solely in the university, the French *inspecteur-général* or the German *Studienrat* has actually taught in schools.

The renewal of language teaching has been slow in coming to Western Europe. But the movement now seems irreversible. It has been claimed that communication is the essential element in all theories of education. Those who have added to their fund of knowledge and skills not only competence in their mother tongue and in mathematics, which is, so to speak, the symbolic language of science, but also the new dimension of thinking that proficiency in a foreign language gives, will have a moral and material advantage over their fellows. If present portents are to be trusted the new Europeans of the 1970s may well have achieved just this.

CHAPTER 1—NOTES

(1) For further details see Appendix, p. 102.

(2) In Italy in 1966–67 almost equal numbers were studying English and French (although slightly more were studying English, and in the *liceo scientifico* it was by far the more popular language); under 10 per cent in the *licei* were studying German, and under 1 per cent, Spanish— cf. *L'Educazione Linguistica: Prima ricerca sulle condizioni dell'insegnamento delle lingue moderne in Italia*, Fratelli Palombri (Rome, 1968, p. 305 and Table 13, p. 622). This work is the most up-to-date study of modern-language teaching in Italy, where progress in the past few years has been rapid.

(3) Cf. *Osteuropa* (Stuttgart, December 1967).

(4) The 129th Plenary Session of the Permanent Conference of German Ministers of Education recommended that languages other than English should be more widely taught.

(5) U. Dahllöf, *Kraven på gymnasiet* (Stockholm, 1965).

(6) V. Gatenby; quoted in L. A. Hill, *Selected Articles on the Teaching of English as a Foreign Language* (London, 1967), p. 91.

(7) *Education in Germany* (No. 4/68, April 1968, Inter Nationes, Bonn).

(8) "L'enseignement des langues vivantes exige de nouvelles méthodes", *Le Monde*, September 13th, 1966.

(9) W. Kölle, *The teaching of English in German High Schools* (*PMLA*, April 1956), p. 26.

Chapter 2
The Goals of Modern-language Teaching

The method of teaching a foreign language and the content of a language course are plainly functions of the aims and objectives of teaching the subject. They must vary according to the goals expressed, and according to the emphasis that is placed on each particular goal. Until recently the main arguments about modern-language teaching had centred more particularly round method; a realization that any method automatically implied a limitation of linguistic content changed slightly the focus of debate. Eventually, however, experts in Western Europe have been forced back to the even more fundamental question: why teach modern languages at all? They found that this question needed answering with great precision, because on the answer so much else depended. It is now generally recognized that in teaching a modern language *aims*—here used specifically to designate long-term goals—and *objectives*—used to designate short-term goals —must be spelt out very exactly. It is also becoming generally accepted that, whilst one may formulate a general set of objectives, the special stress to be placed on each one will depend on the type of education, the type of pupil, and the ultimate destination of that pupil in further education or employment. In short, objectives are also a function of aims.

The aims of learning a foreign language in secondary school may be very briefly and generally summarized. They are clearly to equip the individual with a cognitive or affective apparatus that will serve him in some way either for any subsequent stage of education he may enter, or in his future occupation, or for the enjoyment of leisure. In so far as the individual who becomes so endowed disposes a skill of value to society either in economic terms or in terms of happiness for other people, learning a foreign language has a social purpose. Such general aims are, of course, common to many, if not all, subjects taught in the secondary school. But, again, the emphasis on each particular aim will vary according to the degree to which it is required to be fulfilled.

The objectives of learning a foreign language may be stated more specifically. Table 5 (page 26) gives a summary of the expressed aims and objectives in a number of Western European countries, as they have emerged from a study of official directives and instructions, from surveys and personal interviews. Since the prime object of language is communication, there is universal agreement that languages must be learnt for the acquisition of communication skills: the understanding of speech at normal speed, speaking with an understandable pronunciation and intonation, reading with ease and understanding, and writing the foreign language fluently, idiomatically, and accurately. Since perfection in these skills, even in the mother tongue, is almost out of reach, the minimum criterion for the teacher to strive for is understandability—the capacity to communicate.

Other objectives noted, although some would be accepted readily by countries which do not formally subscribe to them, are not so universally mentioned. One 'mixed' skill—'mixed' because it requires ability in both the source and the target languages—the capacity to translate, commands little support. Yet, as will be seen, at the academic secondary level it is still widely used in many countries as a teaching and a testing device. On the linguistic side knowledge of vocabulary and grammar *per se*—i.e., as part of the general linguistic knowledge of the child—is not very highly prized. On the other hand, knowledge of the linguistic area, its civilization and culture, no less than the pupil's ability to read literary, scientific, and cultural texts in the foreign language, commands broad support. Some half of the countries of Western Europe esteem that the learning of a foreign language has a broader role to plan than the immediate one, since it should contribute to the inner enrichment of the pupil and the development of his personality. Significantly, because it lays great stress upon the promotion of internationalism through the school, West Germany hopes that learning a foreign language may also serve a political end, leading ultimately to an understanding of the characteristics and cultural heritage that constitute the common patrimony of European nations. (In fairness, however, it must be stated that familiarity with foreign nations and their culture may lead to disdain rather than approval; this argument is developed later when dealing with how the foreign culture should be treated.)

One rather striking omission from this catalogue of objectives is the assertion that knowledge of foreign languages helps the pupil to have a better understanding of his mother tongue. This argument was much in vogue when it was used by defenders of the classics,

Table 5—The aims and objectives of modern-language teaching

	Bg(1)	Cy(1)	Dk	Fi(6)	Fr	Ge	Ir	It	Lux	Ma	Neth(12)	Sp(13)	Tu(14)	UK(E)
1. Understanding of speech at normal speed	×	×	×		×	×	×		×(10)	×	×	×	×	×
2. Speaking foreign language with good pronunciation and intonation	×	×	×		×	×	×		×(10)	×	×	×	×	×
3. Reading with ease and understanding	×	×	×		×	×	×		×(10)	×	×	×	×	×
4. Good idiomatic expression in writing	×	×	×	×	×	×	×		×(10)	×	×	×	×	
5. Knowledge of grammar	×	×	×		×	×	×	×(9)	×(10)	×	×		×	
6. Vocabulary									×(10)			×		
7. Ability to translate						×(4)	×(8)		×(10)				×(15)	
8. Communication					×	×								
9. Knowledge of literary, scientific, or cultural texts			×		×			×(9)	×(10)				×	
10. Knowledge of foreign country, its civilization and culture	×	×	×		×	×	×					×	×	×
11. Inner enrichment of pupil, culturally, through contact with life and thought of a foreign country									(×)(10)					(×)(16)
12. Development of personality					×	×								
13. Understanding of common features of European nations						×							×	
14. Political knowledge						×								
15. Knowledge required for career and/or exams	×(2)	×(3)	×(7)	×(7)		×(5)	×		×(11)				×	×(17)

NOTES

(1) Belgium and Cyprus mention that the aims of modern-language teaching as recommended at the Council of Europe Conference held in Ostia in 1966 (approximately equivalent to 1–4 and 10 above) have been incorporated in the regulations of the teaching of languages, but they do not actually list these aims.

(2) Practical use in business and at university level.

(3) English is required for appointment to Government posts and in banks and commercial firms. Many sixth-formers sit for England-based examinations.

(4) Knowledge of specialized 'registers' (*e.g.*, literary, technical, etc.).

(5) Examinations.

(6) Finland mentions in its objectives that hitherto, through the influence of the terminal examination, written skills have been stressed, but that the reform in schools is producing changes.

(7) For university studies.

(8) To and from the language.

(9) *Licei scientifici.*

(10) Everyday usage of the language (morphology, syntax, vocabulary, intonation, style, authors, and civilization).

(11) To prepare pupils for studies in universities in French-, German-, and English-speaking countries.

(12) Netherlands: written expression is required only in the 'economics' type of secondary school.

(13) It may be said that the official directives favour comprehension and oral expression but that "it is the terminal examination which deforms the teaching because it insists in the first place on translation".

(14) Turkey mentions that reforms in progress emphasize reading, writing, and comprehension skills.

(15) Into Turkish only.

(16) "To consider [the language] as a key to the culture of the people whose language it is."

(17) Entrance to institutions of higher education.

and is surely relevant today when advances have been made in the field of contrastive linguistics.

It may be argued that aims and objectives, so expressed, remain no more than pious platitudes. If, for example, the aim is for the foreign language to be of use in higher education we need to know with much more precision what the needs of higher education in languages are. Before the survey previously mentioned as undertaken by Dahllöf in Sweden could be replicated elsewhere, 'feedback' is required from institutions of higher and further education, as well as from employers, as to whether the linguistic ability developed already is proving adequate for their purposes.

In any case, it is surely otiose to set down goals unless they are further analysed into *operational* objectives. At the school level these

will be dictated in part by psychological and pedagogical requirements—the degree of maturation of the pupil, his intellectual
capacity, the need to integrate the goals into the requirements of a
general education. Nevertheless such an analysis may be made either
empirically or pedagogically. A pragmatic procedure might take the
form of a 'situations approach', a 'job' or 'task' analysis. One dis-
covers, for example, by actual observation, what are the lexis or
grammatical structures required by the future foreign-exchange clerk
who may have daily to telephone London in English. A bank official,
for instance, might require to know French in order to be able to
talk to his opposite number in Paris by telex or telephone; to give
the gist of a letter; to explain to a French tourist how he should cash
his travellers' cheques, etc. 'Job analysis' would take this kind of
'situations approach' one stage further. The export manager who is
constantly travelling the Continent for orders would be required to
write out in English a complete list of the vocabulary and structures
which he most frequently requires. These could be translated, but
the register employed would be such that it was 'tailored' to suit the
status and even the personality of the person using them. Both
processes aim in fact at establishing a kind of occupational inventory
or *Berufsbild*. At school level such procedures would doubtless be
over-specific: one accepts, for example, that 'commercial English'
can be learnt only after first learning English *tout court*. Thus the
strictly pedagogical approach would aim at establishing a more
complete analysis of each general objective in turn in order to
establish a minimum of competencies in the different skills or areas
of knowledge. Such an approach, as will be seen, reduces objectives
to a manageable set of classroom tasks to be covered—in fact, a
complete programme of work.

One such inventory of competencies has been established, for the
four communication skills mentioned as objectives, by a group of
European inspectors and teachers.(1) Thus, for the understanding of
speech at normal speed (perhaps, in English, what Daniel Jones
designated as "slower colloquial"), it would be necessary for the
pupil to grasp what was being said by a young and an old person, a
male and a female voice, in—for English—Received Pronunciation
or General American. For listening comprehension the pupil should
be able to follow one voice reading a news item or a literary text, a
public announcement, a telephone message, a popular talk, or a
speech. He should also be able to follow a multivoice communication, such as a conversation on an everyday topic, an interview, a
discussion, or an excerpt from a play. Such comprehension should
not be impeded by everyday characteristics of speech such as interruption, overlapping voices, hesitation, or anacolouthon. As a proof

that he could speak the language intelligibly, the pupil should be required to read aloud a summary compiled by himself or someone else, or be able to give a short talk based on his own notes or on a skeleton outline provided, or even without notes of any kind, in the form of an *exposé*. In participatory communication he might be required to engage in a dialogue on a prepared topic, attend an interview either as interlocutor or interviewee, and join in a general discussion or debate. The skill of reading with ease and understanding (here defined as being also able to appreciate content) might be exercised on graded passages of a literary or non-literary nature, or even on an extensive reading of whole texts. Finally, written expression is also a skill that can be defined with greater precision. It might require, for example, the reproduction of a sequential action read to the pupil, who would be allowed to make notes during the reading. He should be capable of making adequate written summaries in the foreign language of information or arguments either read or heard, with notetaking permitted. He should also be capable of sustained prose-writing of a narrative, descriptive, or discursive kind, whether in the form of composition, essay, or letter-writing. Written work might take the form of a written interpretation of pictorial, statistical, graphical, and diagrammatic data, or the expansion of a skeleton outline, or even the writing of long essays, as part of course work, dealing with the culture and civilization of the foreign country. Many of these exercises will, of course, be out of the range of all but the very intelligent pupils. But such an attempt to define with greater precision what the pupil is capable of doing in the foreign language is obviously of greater value than mere statements of principle. There is no doubt that this 'operationalization' of objectives, graded according to the level of ability and attainment, is the next step to be taken in Western Europe to spelling out more exactly the 'content' of language teaching. Thus, in this way, proceeding from goal analysis to operational objectives, it should be possible to specify units of work suitable for a given age or ability of pupil. The rationale behind this must surely be to systematize language teaching in the same way as other 'skill' subjects, such as mathematics, already are.

One further step that must clearly be taken is to 'weight' objectives according to each pupil's need—in other words, to individualize instruction as much as possible. At the top secondary level, for example, the future university science student requires above all to have a mastery of reading skills; the future student of the interpreter school, on the other hand, requires above all a mastery of the spoken language. Whereas at the lower level the sequential process of listening, speaking, reading, and writing requires to be fairly closely observed, when general curriculum differentiation begins the various skills and kinds of knowledge imparted in the modern-language courses also require to be differentiated. This is surely implicit in the statement made by the assembled language experts of Western Europe at Ostia in 1967, which concluded that "the development of these aims should be integrated in the teaching at all levels *in terms of the age, ability, and interests of the pupils*",(2) (present writer's italics).

There is no doubt that this statement must hold true for knowledge no less than for skills. If an objective is knowledge of the foreign country, then, as the French point out,(3) this must be fostered by the study of texts taken from first-class writers and chosen for their literary, human, and social value. (Where many would part company with the French is when they assert that this choice should not normally exceed more than forty pages thoroughly explained!) Likewise, if foreign languages should promote better international understanding, then 'content' to this end must be chosen. At present there are few signs that this is systematically being done in Western Europe.

Nevertheless for the first time it may be said that in aims and objectives the educational authorities of Western Europe are increasingly in agreement.

CHAPTER 2—NOTES

(1) At a conference on "Continuous assessment in upper secondary education" organized by the Council of Europe at Sundsvall, Sweden, July 1969.

(2) At a conference organized by the Council of Europe at Ostia, Italy, May 1967.

(3) *Instructions* of July 30th, 1965, No. 65–296, Ministère de l'Education Nationale, Paris.

Chapter 3
The Contribution of Linguistics to Language Teaching

Linguistics as a science did not, asserts Georges Mounin, merely "burst like a clap of thunder in a cloudless sky".(1) Yet, such is the relative isolation in which language teachers have hitherto worked—with comparatively little contact on the European plane until recent years, and, as regards English teaching, even less among those who taught the language in Africa and Asia and those who taught it on the Continent—that the findings of linguistic science had until recently been ignored or neglected. The language teacher had held that, after academic training, his domain was the classroom. Now, in preparation for the classroom task, the teacher trainer is attempting to give students at least a background knowledge of linguistics. Some of the discoveries of linguistics have already altered the whole course of language teaching. One of the most striking findings, for example, was that revealed in *Le Français Fondamental*, *Premier Degré*: half of all the language spoken in conversation by Frenchmen was based on some thirty-seven lexical items, and almost all French conversation could be encompassed in some 1300 words! Thus, after some initial resistance, based perhaps on the assumption that teaching was solely an art, teachers in Europe are beginning to realize the utility of linguistic research. The analogy is perhaps with medicine, the practice of which is likewise an art, but which has firm roots in the biological sciences.

The most important feature of linguistics, the concentration on the spoken rather than the written word—de Saussure's *la parole* rather than *la langue*—is now the norm throughout most of Western Europe. The communication aspect, based on speech and essentially instrumentalist and utilitarian, is now the point of departure for the vast majority of language teachers. At the same time particular branches of linguistics are increasingly recognized to be relevant to the classroom. Descriptions of the foreign language, structural-functional analyses of it, identification of contrastive and comparative

31

elements between the source language and the foreign language—all may have classroom applications: the study of structure, function, code, and system can be used in teaching in terms of patterns, grammar, vocabulary, and syntax. Similar use may be made of the discoveries of phonology. Furthermore, the relatively more recent branches of the science, concerned with sociolinguistics and psycholinguistics, may also be of service to the teacher. The effect of linguistics, although oblique because reflected mainly in teaching methods and materials, is nevertheless considerable.

The speed at which innovation occurs must inevitably depend on the pace at which the massive research needed can take place. There is, for example, a shortage of really exhaustive descriptions of the main world languages. The most comprehensive analysis of English being made is that in progress undertaken by Professor Quirk at London University, whose *Survey of English Usage*, when completed, will be authoritative. *Le Français Fondamental*, although a less ambitious project, has proved very useful to teachers because it set down a minimal French largely based on speech. At Mannheim Professor Hugo Moser is working on a project which will perform the same function for German. In the Netherlands, at the University of Utrecht, work is proceeding also for English: an analysis of half a million words of written English has been made, and a similar task is being undertaken for spoken English. In both cases the vocabulary has been limited to an analysis of lexis since 1945, specialized lexis has been omitted, and words and collocations have been distinguished only according to their most usual meanings. From this survey already has been evolved a first-year course in English for Dutch schoolchildren, in which the vocabulary to be retained for use amounts to 500 words.

This limitation of receptive vocabulary is significant. It is, in fact, this principle of limitation which linguistics has introduced into language teaching. In England the Nuffield Project in Foreign Languages is likewise based on vocabulary and structural counts. Among other European countries, Cyprus, France, West Germany, Greece, Norway, and Sweden also state that they control vocabulary for English teaching in this way. The desire for a fresh look at vocabulary arose from the increasing dissatisfaction felt with Michael West's *General Service List*. This, although it had done useful pioneer duty, was based in part on a previous American word-list, was founded on written material, and has a strong bias to literature. (It must be stated that there is some evidence, however, from the teaching of English to immigrants in England that vocabulary control is of lesser importance than the control of structural and functional groups.) Unfortunately the work of descriptive linguistics, which is of course not confined to lexis or 'grammar', but must necessarily include the study of sound-patterns, phonology, orthography, contextual meaning, and the varieties of the language as well, is hampered by lack of funds, although the use of computer techniques could speed analysis considerably.

Until descriptive linguistics can advance, contrastive and comparative linguistics, to which the former feeds prime data, must likewise be held up. Robert Lado's *Linguistics across Cultures*, which dates from as early as 1957, hypothesized that the most effective language learning occurs when the material of instruction is based upon a comparison and a contrast of the native and foreign language:

> Textbooks should be graded as to grammatical structure, pronunciation, vocabulary, and cultural content. And grading can be done best after the kind of comparison we are presenting here.(2)

He gives a few simple examples of what he means: he compares, for example, the sound systems of English and Spanish, listing those English phonemes that are non-existent in Spanish.(3) Since Lado the Center for Applied Linguistics of the Modern Language Association of America has produced a series of volumes setting out the differences and similarities between English and German, Italian and Spanish. A volume comparing English and French has still to appear. Elsewhere other contrastive studies are in progress. For English a notable one is the Stuttgart Project on Applied Contrastive Linguistics (PAKS) under the direction of Professor Nickel. Nickel has summed up the task of applied contrastive linguistics as follows:

> (It) . . . does not aim at drawing the pupil's attention constantly and systematically to language contrasts. Its objective is rather to aid the textbook author in collecting and arranging his material, and to help the teacher in presenting his subject-matter. Both author and teacher require a knowledge of contrastive grammar in order to be able to predict, explain, correct, combat, and eliminate errors due to interference between source and target language.(4)

According to Nickel, contrastive linguistics has responsibility for the didactic programming of subject-matter—*what* shall be taught—but the teacher remains responsible for the methodological programming —*how* it shall be taught.

The task of contrastive linguistics is immense because, for English alone, in Western Europe, it would mean comparing and contrasting in their most significant aspects no fewer than fourteen different languages. A number of part studies have been completed, and many are under way. Meanwhile, in awaiting results, some substitute must be found. The experienced language teacher has always realized that mistakes in the foreign language frequently—but not always—arise because of 'interference' from the mother tongue. The process of 'error analysis' needs to be systematized on an international basis. For example, the mastery of English is undoubtedly more difficult to achieve for some nationalities than for others. This 'difficulty factor' (which may of course relate to other variables such as motivation) has never been sufficiently analysed. Pending the large-scale and exhaustive evaluations of contrastive linguistics, one procedure might be for international panels of language teachers to enumerate the difficulties, and to see whether any patterns of error emerged: are the obstacles to be overcome by the Frenchman or Italian in learning English characteristic of the Romance-language speaker; are they identifiable similarly for the Germanic-language speaker? Such international 'error analyses' might stimulate the creation of suitable means to overcome the difficulties by the devising of, for example, pattern drills, pronunciation exercises, etc. This would be at least a palliative.

One of the most important contributions of sociolinguistics to language learning has been to make the teacher more aware of the fact of 'register'—the 'variety of language according to use'. Halliday illustrates this point cogently:

> There is no need to labour the point that a sports commentary, a church service, and a school-lesson are linguistically quite distinct. One sentence from these and many more such situation types would enable us to identify it correctly. We know, for example, where "an early announcement is expected" comes from, and "apologies for absence were received"; these are not simply free variants of "we ought to hear soon" and "was sorry he couldn't make it".(5)

He goes on to remark that ". . . up to now we know very little about the various registers of spoken English". He suggests a tentative taxonomy of registers according to: (a) the 'field of discourse'—the physical area of language activity, (b) the 'mode of discourse'— spoken or written forms, such as the language of newspapers, medicine, etc., (c) the 'style of discourse',—a result of how the participants regard each other, whether formally or informally.

It is clear that the appropriate registers of language to be used will depend on the situation, the particular subject of conversation, and the person who is being addressed. A good example of how register is being tackled is in the devising of the German course for the Schools Council Foreign Languages Teaching Materials Project at York University. The language used in the course is selected so that pupils may carry out a 'linguistic activity'. This assumes an intention or purpose, such as how to express likes or dislikes, how to buy and sell, how to make excuses or apologies. The members of the team preparing the course first decided what *they* would say in such circumstances, and also recorded conversations with Germans who were actually engaged in those activities. The choice was finally made of material from these data—not, however, by members of the team, but by teachers of German, who selected what they considered to be the most appropriate for their own pupils. It is clearly an urgent task for all language teachers to limit or define the registers of the language they need to teach. If the advanced student is learning the language in order merely to read and write the prose of argument, then clearly the register of discursive prose must be the norm. More probably, some pedagogical compromise needs to be arrived at—even the young person of sixteen learning English may not finally have decided whether he requires the language in order to read poetry or to interpret engineering blueprints! There must be a new look at what Martin Goos termed the "style matrix" and divided into five main categories: intimate, casual, consultative, formal, and frozen.(6) Most teachers in Western Europe are aware of the problem, but pending the results of research are at a loss as to how to tackle it.

Special problems of urgency may likewise be singled out in the field of psycholinguistics, which is becoming in many Western European countries one of the main concerns of the teacher trainer. Since much of language learning depends initially upon memorization, one such problem is concerned with how short-term learning may be converted into long-term learning, so that what has once been learnt may not be forgotten. Patrick Suppes has adduced evidence to show that if learning occurs at a faster rate than forgetting, then the main emphasis in teaching should always be on new materials. If this hypothesis is accepted, then in language teaching the 'whole method', in which a body of new material is worked through completely, may be better than the 'part method'. At present the general practice in European schools would appear to favour the 'part method', in which a new concept must be thoroughly known before moving on to a fresh one. On the other hand, if Suppes is correct, the at present haphazard, trial-and-error methods of determining the optimal rate at which new material should be introduced and revised later are not sufficient. Certain countries, for example, lay down that the 'grammar' of English must be covered over a certain period of years—in West Germany (North Rhine-Westphalia), for example, four years, between 11 and 15, is specified. This may be unduly long, and capable of being reduced by the use of audio-visual courses.

In one important respect the findings of psycholinguistics have been translated into classroom terms. Research has shown that meaningfulness ('contextualization') encourages learning and retention. A move has therefore been made recently to concentrate upon giving meaning to structural drills, and to arrange them in a logical sequence of context. This was a consideration too often neglected in the early years of audio-lingual and audio-visual courses, which relied more on habit and the inculcating of automatisms and less on the ability to understand. But since ultimately the teacher can only be the presenter of ways of learning, each pupil will learn to speak the language in the way that suits him best, either through habit-formation or contextualization of subject-matter. It is nevertheless important that courses combine both elements.

It is difficult to measure exactly what has been the impact of linguistics on the European classroom. It is certain, however, that it has been significant. It has brought about a recategorization of the objectives of language learning, a refinement of teaching materials, from the grading of vocabulary to a more systematic introduction of structures, and a re-thinking of method in general. This impact is likely to increase in force as linguistic knowledge increases and is applied in the schools.(7)

CHAPTER 3—NOTES

(1) G. Mounin, *Clés pour la linguistique* (Paris, 1969).

(2) R. Lado, *Linguistics across Cultures* (1957), p. 3.

(3) R. Titone has also carried out studies of the difficulties experienced by Italian pupils in perceiving the phonological features of English and French. He concludes that further research is essential to establish correlations between ear, ethnic origin, age, sex, and degree of linguistic sophistication. The research is reported in R. Titone's "Difficulties on the part of Italian younger adolescents in the perception of some phonological features of the English and French languages", *Orientamenti Pedagogici*, viii, 4, 1961.

(4) G. Nickel, *Contrastive Linguistics and Foreign Language Teaching*, Paper read at the Second International Conference of Applied Linguistics (Cambridge, 1969).

(5) M. A. K. Halliday, "The Users and Uses of Language", in J. A. Fishman's (ed.), *Readings in the Sociology of Language* (The Hague, 1968), pp. 139 *et seq*.

(6) M. Goos, *The Five Clocks* (1962).

(7) An authoritative publication on the applications of linguistics to modern languages is *New Trends in Linguistic Research* (Council for Cultural Co-operation of the Council of Europe, Strasbourg, 1963).

Chapter 4

The Teaching of the Foreign Culture and Civilization

It is a truism to say that language is a key, but at a time when the instrumental objective of communication is considered paramount it is perhaps worthwhile to repeat the viewpoint of C. C. Fries:

> To deal with the culture and life of a people is not just an adjunct of a practical language course, something alien and apart from its main purpose, but an essential feature of every stage of language learning.

At school level 'culture' is used loosely to describe the life, the civilization, and the literature of the area whose language is being studied. A more precise definition is that given by Oeckel, who defines it as "the interaction of race, domicile, economy, science, philosophy, law, the form of the state, art, religion, customs, and language."(1) Such a definition requires to be supplemented by one that takes also into account the affective as well as the cognitive attitudes that can be induced by the study of a foreign language. Oakeshott defines culture more broadly as an

> inheritance of feelings, emotions, images, visions, thoughts, beliefs, ideas, understandings, intellectual and practical enterprises, languages, relationships, organizations, canons and maxims of conduct, procedures, rituals, skills, works of art, books, musical compositions, tools, artifacts, and utensils.(2)

So defined culture is a mode of common discourse shared by a group of people who form a cultural entity, but who may or may not share a common language.

Oeckel recommends that for the teaching of the culture of the English-speaking world there should be concentration on its great political and social problems, on its power of extension, and on its basic inner motivating forces. This recommendation throws us back to the definition of a cultural entity. Is there, in fact, any entity that might be described as the 'English-speaking world' or for that matter a 'French-speaking' or 'German-speaking' one? The tacit assumption behind the assertion—perhaps not entirely unjustified—is that communality of language implies a communality of culture. Undoubtedly, one may speak of common cultural origins, but the force of diversification between, say, Britain and North America has surely been so strong that it is now almost impossible to speak of a common discourse of culture, save in the most general sense of the term. To accept the concept that *Sprachgebiet* is synonomous with *Kulturgebiet* is to accept the theory that lay behind British imperialism, where a common language implied a common ethos, or Pan-Germanism, or French cultural chauvinism which sees Quebec as the child too long deprived of its mother. It plainly cannot be in this sense that the term cultural entity is to be understood.

In any case, when one attempts to spell out in operational terms what form the study of culture and civilization in relation to modern languages might take an even greater precision is required. Eva Sivertsen(3) has made a useful categorization as follows:

1. Physical and economic geography.
2. History of the people and country.
3. Political and social institutions and patterns.
4. Educational philosophy, traditions, and institutions.
5. Religious life and institutions.
6. The philosophy and the philosophers of culture.
7. The literature.
8. Other written or printed forms of communication: newspapers and advertisements, laws and regulations, business and informal letters, etc.
9. Other forms of artistic expression, such as architecture, sculpture, painting, and music.
10. The pattern of life, daily routine, interests, and hobbies of the people.

This list is, of course, not exhaustive: it omits, for example, the study of the scientific and technological, as well as of the industrial, commercial, and financial life of the foreign country.

From this amorphous mass of possibilities how is the language teacher to select, because the encyclopaedic nature of his material necessitates choice? In works such as *Guide France*, by Guy Michaud, Director of the *Centre de Recherche de l'Enseignement de la Civilisation* (CERC), the teacher can select. The principle of selection must be surely to choose what is characteristic or typical, relating the topics to other subjects that are studied in school. This is in accordance with the German curriculum theory of *exemplarische Lehre*, in which it is recognized that every topic can have only *paradigmatic* significance. Lado, in *Linguistics across Cultures*, speaks of contrastive cultural studies. This should perhaps be the key to teaching method, although it is probably well to stress to children that the sum of phenomena appearing in Western cultures which are similar is infinitely greater than the sum total of the dissimilar.

Moreover, it is essential that cultural information be graded in the same way as linguistic information. It can, of course, be taught in many ways only marginally related to the classroom—and consequently possibly more interesting: project work, out-of-school activities, school journeys, use of the library and a documentation centre, drama and cinema productions, drawing upon the services of 'assistants', or even arranging group exchanges of pupils for whole terms. All these are means of ensuring that the visual images presented to the pupils are kept up to date. The image of the Frenchman with black spade beard, dressed in morning-suit and spats, still survives in the minds of many middle-aged Englishmen from the textbook pictures of their schooldays. Even the note of authenticity given by audio-visual courses may become outdated: the clothes of the pictures of *Voix et Images* appear strange to the miniskirted girls and informally dressed youngsters of today. Few Englishmen realize that doubledecker buses on Parisian streets are now commonplace. The teacher must be beware of imprinting inexact notions of the foreign country on the child's mind. As yet we have little idea of how this mental picture of the foreign country is formed, nor how stereotypes and prejudices, either favourable or unfavourable, are implanted.

That the dangers of wrong mental pictures being formed do exist is perhaps evidenced by a study of examination papers in English set in various countries abroad. Passages of English for translation or commentary in recent years have dealt, for example, with London clubs, which are surely more typical of Edwardian times than today. Another passage mentions "dressing for dinner", which the candidate has to explain, and a footnote adds: "An Englishman even today sometimes dresses for dinner." Yet another examination paper set for commentary a passage drawn from a rather obscure work by Robert Louis Stevenson. If the images that these passages summon up are rather old-fashioned one must be just as wary of reflecting falsely what is allegedly contemporary. An examination test in one country required candidates to write a letter to a newspaper refuting another letter already published, very slangy and trivial in tone, and certainly not of the type to be found in a serious newspaper. London is larger than Clubland or even Carnaby Street, and English literary achievement greater than minor Victoriana or even the 'gutter Press'. If the teacher of languages has obvious difficulties in keeping himself up to date his difficulties in striking the just mean with his pupils are no less apparent.

Fischer-Wollpert(4) has drawn attention to the great difficulty encountered in providing a balanced picture through selected reading of the cultural life of a people, or a reading which is rich and varied enough to enable the pupil to come to an informed personal judgment. There is a danger that the teacher will produce the image of a national stereotype which falsifies reality (although it must be admitted that some stereotypes do in fact exist). In any case the culture of a people does not consist only in positive traits. Just how far is a teacher justified in drawing attention to the negative, darker side of a people's cultural heritage? Schubel(5) claims that after the First World War there were English-language teachers in Germany who taught about the negative as well as the positive facets of English culture: 'cant' in English political, religious, and social life, the deprecable aspects of Puritanism, and the snobbery associated with the 'gentleman ideal'. In Nazi Germany the official line was at first to propagate the alleged 'cousin' relationship between the English and German peoples—at least until the outbreak of the Second World War, when the less laudable aspects of English character were emphasized. Perhaps, as for the teaching of history, the modern-languages teacher can only be as honest and as impartial as possible, stressing that other nations think and express themselves differently.

In any case some cultural distortion must undoubtedly take place. A literary example may illustrate this. It comes almost as a shock to the English-speaking person to realize the high esteem in which Edgar Allan Poe is held in France, or to learn that the novels of Charles Morgan have been more widely read on the other side of the Channel than in his own country. There are, of course, cogent reasons for these preferences: Poe's influence on Baudelaire, or the undoubted mastery that the French possess of the *roman psychologique* in their own literature. It is at least arguable that in the European context each country should identify those elements of the foreign culture that it considers of special relevance for its own pupils. The Germans have paid the English-speaking world, for example, the compliment of looking at its political ideas, and have considered the possibility of using selective material on them in modern languages for the political education of young Germans. At another level there are also convinced Europeanists on the Continent who consider, if Europe is to be united, the insistence must be on English rather than American culture. Despite these special cases, one would do well to consider whether there is not a basic minimum of a foreign culture that *all* children, regardless of nationality, should be made aware of.

If teachers were available it might be appropriate to introduce new interdisciplinary courses at the upper academic secondary level which might, for example, consist of 'English Studies', 'French Studies', or 'German Studies'. Such courses given in the foreign language would attempt to study in a systematic way the contemporary history, geography, literature, current affairs, and social life of the English- or French- or German-speaking world. Their scope might be further enlarged to take account of the future career of the pupils, and include such subjects as law, economics, science, and technology. This would give a content to language courses at this level which they too often lack. For future translators, interpreters, international civil servants, and foreign-office officials, as well as future businessmen, a further development might be a course in 'European Studies' where the content would be similar, but on a European scale, and taught using all three of the main languages of Western Europe—English, French, and German.

The practice of teaching the culture of the foreign country, particularly its history and geography, in the mother tongue is surely only permissible with beginners in order to stimulate interest and motivate. The practice in England, where even at university level lectures, for example, on German history, intended as a necessary background for the literature course, are given in *English*, strikes most other countries as being objectionable and defeating its own object.

In practice most European countries do not teach about the foreign culture in any systematic fashion. Table 6 summarizes the non-literary content of the language courses in a number of West European countries. Although the French programme for the *lycée* prescribes British authors of the eighteenth, nineteenth, and twentieth centuries for the penultimate class, and American authors for the top grade, it gives great liberty in the choice of texts to be studied—the exercise of *explication de texte* is widely used in this kind of study. In West Germany (Hessen) the syllabus at the upper academic secondary level (which is at present under review) recommends the reading of a variety of texts of a philosophical, religious, scientific, historical, political, and socio-economic kind. The recommended authors range from Burke to Toynbee. In addition much contemporary prose—not *belles lettres*—is available, and political speeches and newspapers are also studied. In Denmark and Sweden the stress is almost entirely on contemporary civilization—mostly articles on education, political institutions, law, and everyday life. The recommended authors are mainly modern, with a notable exception of Shakespeare. This emphasis on the contemporary scene is now apparent practically everywhere. Only in England, where G.C.E. examining boards lay

Table 6—The non-literary content (civilization, culture, etc.) of language courses

Country	Are there any official directives for teaching non-literary content?	Notes
Belgium	Yes	Use of reviews, newspapers, anthologies, recommended. In the *sections commerciales* business letters and documents.
Cyprus	No	Material to schools from British Council, U.S. Information Service, and the *Centre Culturel Français.*
Denmark	Yes	From 50 to 100 pages describing contemporary civilization—mostly articles on education, political institutions, law, everyday life, etc. Similar information given as a running commentary to any text studied. Use of newspapers in lessons also encouraged.
Federal Republic of Germany	Yes	1957 syllabus (under review) recommends reading of philosophical, religious, scientific, historical, political, and social-economic prose. Authors recommended, *inter alia*, are: Burke, Mill, James Madison, A. Hamilton, Oliver Wendell Holmes, Toynbee, Montesquieu, Voltaire, Rousseau. Much contemporary non-literary prose is available and political speeches and newspapers are also studied.
Finland	No	Prescribed textbooks may contain such material. Teachers have freedom, but tend to concentrate on language.
France	No	Official programmes on civilization have now been abolished. There are no history or literary courses as such, but much *lecture expliquée* of texts, many of which deal with history and culture of foreign country. In top grade mainly American authors are studied.
Ireland	No	"Pupils should gradually be made acquainted with the life and culture of the people whose language they are learning."
Italy	No	Teachers have free choice.
Luxembourg	No	
Malta	No	In general, matter of this nature is always included. At top level it is compulsory.
Netherlands	No	Textbooks generally contain elements of history, geography, social life, etc.
Spain	Yes	Official directives do not prescribe subject matter; teachers have free choice.
Turkey	Yes	No special teaching aids exist for this purpose.
United Kingdom (England)	No	Teachers have free choice, but suggestions are made in the syllabus.

down the syllabus, is there a series of prescribed texts of a literary nature consisting mainly of what has been termed "an anthology of the dead".

Regarding literary texts, there is in fact still great disagreement in Europe. Their protagonists say that they serve as an introduction to the great literature of the past. Those opposed to them claim, however, that pupils having to prepare for them in examinations read them in translation. Thus there has been a move to substitute modern texts—sometimes less easily available in translation—for classical ones. But in some cases this may merely mean to substitute the trivial for the sublime. The practice of prescribing only a few set books is surely to be condemned because it is unfortunately usually only those that will be read. It is as if one told an art student to look at only one particular masterpiece for two years. The alternative is literary extracts which seem equally unsatisfactory as offering only snippets of the literary culture. A tolerable compromise would seem extensive reading, as rapid as may be, of as many modern works as possible to give the pupil a taste for the foreign literature. But he must have neither a surfeit of one diet nor tantalizing and unsatisfying morsels of the other. The aim must be to whet his appetite for further study in higher education. It is difficult, however, to convince the English, with their predilection for set books, or the French, with their delight in *morceaux choisis*, of the reasonableness of such procedure. One must be thankful that the rather arid study of literary history *per se* has now been abandoned everywhere.

Despite the difficulties inherent in the study of literature, the most commonly used medium for teaching the culture of the foreign country remains the printed word. It has been said that oral and aural work used as a medium for communicating culture too often results in the pupil merely obtaining the 'small change' of the foreign civilization—"a language must communicate what is worth communicating". This does not rule out films or plays. What is proposed is a thematic approach to the teaching of the culture. Preference should be given obviously to modern writers, but the mere fact of chronological remoteness should not necessarily rule out a text for the brighter pupils. Even today, for example, for the discussion of the freedom of the Press, extracts from Milton's *Areopagitica* might be a useful starting-point. It would obviously lead on to the study of the newspapers of the country itself, as well as to the reading of modern novels which deal with the newspapers. Such a thematic approach to a topic in which reference is made to any material available could be spread over several months.

The preparation of such material should be an international matter. Organizations such as UNESCO have already done much to improve the quality and exactness of history teaching by promoting bilateral and multilateral discussions between historians of different nationalities in order 'to set the record straight'. Might not modern-language teachers, if brought into contact in a similar way, also play a part in developing 'lines of instruction'—even actual lessons and courses for the 'culture and civilization' element in language courses. 'Work kits' which contain reading passages and audio-visual aids of all kinds are required. In the European context this is obviously a field where the Council of Europe could give a lead.

Nevertheless one must recognize that knowledge of the foreign country or countries is best acquired on the spot. To a certain extent ignorance is dispelled today in many practical ways. Cheap travel facilities for young people, no less than the existence of a 'young people's culture' expressed in 'pop' music, movies, and other super-ficialities which transcend national boundaries have paradoxically provided deeper insights into the way foreigners live than can ever be given through school studies.

CHAPTER 4—NOTES

(1) F. Oeckel, *Englische Kulturkunde im Lichte der Unterrichtspraxis* (Leipzig, 1928).
(2) Oakeshott, "Learning and Teaching", in R. S. Peters's (ed.) *The Concept of Education* (London, 1967).
(3) Eva Sivertsen, paper [CCC/EGT(68)3] given at a Council of Europe conference in Oslo in 1967.
(4) H. Fischer-Wollpert, "Das sozialkundliche Prinzip im englischen Unterricht der Oberstufe", *Gesellschaft, Staat, Erziehung* (1956), p. 163.
(5) F. Schubel, *Methodik des Englisch-Unterrichts* (Frankfurt, 2nd edition, 1960), p. 181.

Chapter 5

Teaching and Learning: General Considerations

The increased intensity of language learning in European schools is due not only to its extension to the primary classes in many schools, but also to its reinforcement in the secondary stage. Table 7 shows the total possible 'foreign language exposure' in hours per week in modern languages in the academic secondary school, which is usually where teaching is the most concentrated. It represents mainly the teaching of English as a foreign language, but for comparative purposes approximate figures for the teaching of French in England have also been included. The overall number of period-hours per week ranges from forty-five in West Germany to twelve in Greece. The overall average number of periods is 26·4, with an average per age grade of 3·7. The greatest concentration in language teaching occurs between the ages of 12 and 16, where the overall number of period-hours ranges from twenty-six in Cyprus to ten in Greece. The average number of periods for all countries is 18·6 for this age range. Table 8 below represents a rough calculation of the time in period-hours devoted in the secondary school to the study of the first foreign language in a number of countries. It is divided between the most specialized humanities and the most specialized science section. The extreme variability is due in part to the fact that the study of a foreign language in the secondary school differs greatly in the number of years accorded to it. Yet, while admitting that each national group has its peculiar difficulties in mastering a foreign tongue, the variability from 435 to 1200 hours is extreme.

The data presented show that much research still remains to be done, both as to the optimum age for beginning the learning of a foreign language and also on the frequency and intensity with which teaching is carried out. Nevertheless it is plain that the total 'language exposure' of pupils in European schools has been augmented. Even a decade ago the picture presented would have been vastly different.

A further indicator of the growing importance of languages in the

Table 7—Total possible number of period-hours per week in academic secondary education in modern languages(1)

Country	10	11	12	13	14	15	16	17	18	Total 12–16	Total overall
Au (2)	5	4	3	3	3	3	3	3	3	15	30
Bg	—	—	0	3	3	3	3	3	—	12	15
Cy (3)	—	—	4	5	5	6	6	6	—	26	32
Dk	—	—	—	—	4	3	5	4	4	12	20
Fi	5	5	5	5	5	5	4	4	3	24	41
Fr	—	3	3	3	3	3	3	3	—	15	21
Ge	5	5	5	5	5	5	5	5	5	25	45
Gk	—	2	2	2	2	2	2	—	—	10	12
Ic	—	—	—	5	5	5	5	5	5	20	30
It	—	2	3	3	3	4	3	3	4	16	25
Lux	—	—	5	5	5	4	3	3	—	22	25
Neth	—	—	4	4	4	4	4	—	—	20	20
No	—	—	4	4	4	5	7	8	—	24	32
Sp	—	0	6	4	1	3	1	3	—	15	18
Sd	—	2	5	4	3	3	3	2	4	18	26
Sw	—	3	3	3	3	4	4	4	—	17	24
Tu	—	—	4	3	3	5	4	4	—	19	23
UK(E) (5)	—	5	5	5	4	5	6	6	—	25	36

Notes

(1) A blank (—) does *not* mean that no modern-language teaching takes place at this age, but merely that it does not take place as part of *secondary* education. Where alternatives are given in official documents the higher figure is taken. Malta is excluded because English is one of the official languages, and secondary schools have English as a vehicular language.

(2) From 1971 secondary education in Austria will be a ten-year course.

(3) Cyprus: commercial section.

(4) Sweden: includes six years of *grundskola* (unitary comprehensive education) to age 16.

(5) Figures for England relate to French and are inserted for comparative purposes.

Table 8—Approximate number of period-hours devoted in secondary school to the study of the first foreign language

Country	Humanities Section	Science Section
Bg	720–480	720–480
Cy	720	720
Dk	965	—
Fi	720	720
Fr	700	700
Ge	1200	880
It	—	800
Lux	960–800	800
Neth	435	435
Sp	570	570
Tu	540	540

Table 9—Percentage of time allocated to various subject groups in different countries

Subject Groups	West Germany		Belgium		France		Italy		Luxembourg		Netherlands		U.S.S.R.
	I	II	I	II	I	II	I	II	I	II	I	II	
Maths–Science	21	29	18	26	19	31	13	19	17	28	15	25	33
Languages	46	34	54	37	51	41	53	46	55	41	60	52	33
Other	33	37	28	37	30	28	34	35	28	31	25	23	34
TOTAL	100	100	100	100	100	100	100	100	100	100	100	100	100

West European context is the percentage of time spent on them— whether in the study of the mother tongue, modern languages, or classical languages—as compared with the time spent on mathematical and scientific subjects. Table 9 shows a comparison of the time spent in the academic secondary schools of the Common Market countries and in the U.S.S.R.(1) Column I represents the percentage of school time spent in the most specialized 'humanities' section, and column II that spent in the most specialized 'science' section.

In the Common Market countries the approximate mean proportion of time devoted to languages of all kinds by the pupil specializing in the 'humanities' is some 53 per cent. Even for the pupil specializing in mathematics and science it is as high as 42 per cent. A more recent calculation made for France shows that for the first foreign language alone some 12 per cent of the pupil's time is devoted to it.

Before going on to speak about methods and materials distinctions must first be drawn between the elementary, the intermediate, and the advanced stages of language learning. Yet it is very difficult to define operationally what is meant by each of these three stages. One operational definition might be explained in terms of the number of lexical items that have to be acquired by the end of each stage, but unfortunately many countries do not proceed by means of a vocabulary count. Nor, as we have seen, is it possible to define exactly the three stages in relation to the number of years spent learning a language. In some countries the learning process is more intensive than in others, being carried out over very few years but with a high number of lessons a week.

Yet with the advent of audio-visual and audio-lingual courses procedures and practices in the initial stages of language learning have become increasingly standardized. In general, such courses as those developed by St Cloud or the greatly successful *Passport to English* would appear to be satisfactory for the first two or three years, although the problem of boredom is nevertheless being encountered at this beginning stage. There is no doubt that some elementary courses, and unfortunately those which are based on active methods, contain many trivialities. The result is that pupils are often encouraged to be 'active' in the use of materials which are not worth being 'active' about. One solution to this may be for the pupils to be initiated from the very outset into the culture of the country whose language they are studying, so that the course possesses a 'content' of intrinsic value. Some such procedures are even more necessary in the intermediate stage. There is much evidence that the adolescent may find this kind of course extremely monotonous, despite the fact it may be are pictorially well designed, interesting in

48

content, and sedulously followed up by practical sessions in the language laboratory. It would seem that up to now no country has quite succeeded in resolving this problem, which, of course, is one endemic in the whole of education and not only in modern languages. However, by the upper secondary school intrinsic motivation may have taken over, or the pupils may be motivated by the stimulus of examinations or their career prospects.

For gifted pupils very little is known also as to the comparative efficiency of the various methods advocated. It may well be that the best procedure for teaching a foreign language to a bright child who has already mastered one language other than his own is to practise a policy of total 'immersion' in the language by, say, a course of 300 hours spread over six months. For such a case another possibility, which must not be entirely ruled out, is to teach by the old grammar-translation method, working through a conventional grammar as quickly as possible and then following this by an intensive audio-visual course. Whereas with small children the recipe of 'little and often' would seem empirically to be the most efficient, the contrary may hold true at a later age. Since what the Germans term *Epochen-unterricht* is practised in another subject, which bears some resemblance to language learning—that of mathematics—it may well be that sustained bursts of language learning for days or even months on end are likewise the most rewarding. In any case it would seem ridiculous to do what sometimes still occurs in English grammar schools, and timetable each language period separately for 40 minutes' teaching time. At lower levels opinion seems to agree that three hours a week of language instruction is a minimum, and in this initial stage of learning the pupil should be expected to master at least 100 grammatical patterns and 1000 lexical items. In the intermediate stage the number of instruction hours might well be extended to four a week and the task of learning a further 100 grammatical patterns and 1000 lexical items would seem appropriate.

Increasingly (although not at sixth-form level in England) the medium of instruction is the foreign language itself. The Hamburg Directives for the teaching of English, for example, are typical: "Die Unterrichtssprache ist Englisch." But three exceptions to this rule appear to be general: the mother tongue may be used for grammatical explanations, for clarifying abstract arguments, and for discussing points of style or artistry. This use of the target language as the teaching medium represents one of the most notable advances made over the past decade.

Such advances have been accomplished within the broad framework of a new conception of teaching method which may be described as the 'integral approach'. Renzo Titone has grouped teaching

49

4

methods into three categories which he dubs formal, functional, and integral. The formal method is, as its name implies, the classical or traditional one. The functional method may be of four kinds: the direct method, which should be rejected as being too rigorous and uncompromising; the intensive method, in which a 'tandem' approach of oral and grammar work is adopted for a short period; the 'intuitive' method, under which may be assumed audio-visual courses; and the linguistic method, which is based on a comparative analysis of linguistic forms. The integral method, which is clearly Titone's own preference, attempts to harmonize what is good in the other methods. Titone says:

> a truly complete method [which] . . . ought *to aim at the four basic automatisms* (to speak, to understand by listening, to understand by reading, to write), but relating these in the live context of *real situations*, joining them to the immediate objective of making understood the dimensions and the manners of the culture of the people which speaks the language, and arranging them also in order to arrive at an adequate understanding of the *mentality* and *spiritual outcomes* of the people.(2)

It is this method, which embodies the basic skills, but does not exclude the use of other methods where applicable, and which aims also at contextualization and contact with cultural reality, which is becoming generally acceptable in Western Europe today. How it may be made operational in its linguistic aspects may perhaps be shown in the diagram given below, compiled by a Dutch languages expert, Mr Breitenstein.(3)

TEACHING MATERIAL

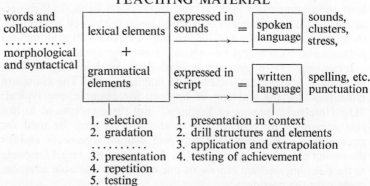

At the lower and intermediate stages of language learning, whether these all fall within secondary education or extend downwards into the primary school, it is the four-dimensional approach of the inculcation of aural, oral, reading, and writing skills which underlies the modern approach to language teaching in Western Europe. Likewise there is general acceptance of the phasing of teaching method in a sequence of presentation, explanation, practice, application, and creative application.

Before going on to exemplify how this works in two countries, Sweden and Belgium, the existence of a strong minority view must be recognized. A small teaching element in every country holds that it *may* not be easier to speak a foreign language first and write it later: the converse may still be true. Moreover, a long period of exclusively oral work *may* not be necessary in the beginning stages of learning a language. This minority view must be respected, if not approved. The verdict on the new methods, although the portents are very favourable, must be that their success is not yet proven. Until a generation of European schoolchildren who have started to learn a foreign language at the age of eight or thereabouts have passed through the complete secondary education course and entered higher education or employment, what some would describe as this reactionary element must be given the benefit of the doubt.

Since the Swedes may well be the most advanced people in the world in their language teaching, the summary of the new directives concerning it which came into force in the autumn of 1970 in the Swedish comprehensive school (ages 7–16) may be interesting.(4) The instructions given firstly enjoin the observance of three principles: *concretization* (*e.g.*, showing a picture or object), *monolingualism* (teaching in the foreign language), realization of the active *relationship between the spoken and the written forms of the foreign language*. As regards *practice*, after the initial stage all communication skills should be practised at every lesson; listening practice should consist of a variety of voices and should almost invariably be combined with conversation practice. Such conversation practice may take a set form or be unstructured. *Set conversation practice* should be employed to stress special forms and structural patterns, and for basic training in words and phrases. Texts in the manual should therefore be used as the starting-point, and all errors should be corrected. *Free conversation practice*, on the other hand, should be used so that the pupil may develop a linguistic imagination, and in it only gross errors should be rectified, and then as unobtrusively as possible. *Pronunciation* should be taught mainly by repetition of speech at the normal rate, with correction and reiteration, and the judicious use of phonetic transcriptions by both teachers and pupils. The more typical characteristics of Standard American should also be taught. *Language patterns* should be taught by giving a large number of examples. Inferences or generalizations regarding them should be made by the pupils and elucidated so far as possible in the foreign language. New patterns should be introduced with discretion, and comprehension of the pattern should not be complicated by introducing it with unfamiliar vocabulary. *Reading* may be either *intensive* or *extensive*, for enjoyment and information. *Writing* should take as wide a variety of forms as possible: replies to questions, pictorial descriptions, texts with questions and exercises, dramatizations, reproduction, summary, letters, and compositions. As far as possible all work should be individualized.

This general example of how a modern language course for, say, the 12–16 year olds should proceed may be supplemented by an example of a method for a similar age group based mainly on audio-visual work and taken from Belgium. The method, as outlined by a well-known Belgian inspector,(5) advocates proceeding from a structuro-global approach to an analytical-synthetical one. It advocates realistic dialogue—not mere artificial question and answer—because this best lends itself to imitation, reconstruction, and exploitation. The first step consists in dealing with the *situation* of the lesson unit entirely orally. It is followed by that of *presentation*, in which there is an integral presentation of a dialogue by tape-recorder and visual aid. This is followed by *explanation* of the dialogue, picture by picture. The forms that explanation can take are many and varied. It is anticipated that this phase will be the one of greatest difficulty for the teacher. A stage of *repetition* then ensues, phrase by phrase, of the entire dialogue. Here the emphasis must be less on phonetical accuracy than on information. Acting on a stimulus-response mechanism, the pupil must eventually be able to recapitulate the whole dialogue correctly when stimulated by the appropriate picture. The order of the pictures should eventually be varied for practice purposes. The pupil when nearly word-perfect should then be able to 'act out' the dialogue. The next, more difficult stage, is that of *exploitation*. This goes beyond the mere 'mim-mem' method: the pupil should now be induced to use the structures and vocabulary in different situations, first in a piecemeal fashion and then as a whole. Again this stage demands considerable ingenuity on the part of the teacher, who must invent situations related to or parallel to the original one. It is followed by a phase of *fixation* in which the pupil has to create for himself short situations, using the original structures, but with different models. This is conceived of as the phase of active grammatical fixation, but is one in which the formulation of rules is to be avoided. The final phase is one of *integration* in which a novel 'situation' is used so as to utilize not only the new linguistic elements just acquired, but also elements learnt previously. This is the stage which represents the beginnings of a real conversation, leading successively to the recounting of a story or the giving of a description, and eventually to written work. This 'written work' phase, however, occurs some six weeks later and acts as revision and consolidation. Using their textbooks, the pupils this time rework the text of the lesson, reading aloud and listening to recordings. They copy out the text, do different exercises upon it, including dictations and other written work. (Dictation is a much neglected exercise. Yet it is one of the best instruments for the creation of automatic written mechanisms, improving comprehension and spelling and fostering grammatical accuracy by practical examples.) Thus the cycle of the lesson unit is completed.

It is generally accepted that time must be rationally distributed at the lower and intermediate levels according to some general principle. One estimate of this distribution of time, which in fact also includes the advanced level, has been suggested(6) as follows:

Table 10—Percentage distribution of time according to level of language learning

Level	Structures	Global Comprehension	Vocabulary Acquisition	Literary and Cultural Texts
Beginners	80	20 (1)	—	—
Intermediate	$33\frac{1}{3}$	$33\frac{1}{3}$	$33\frac{1}{3}$ (3)	—
Advanced	10	30 (2)	30 (4)	30

(1) aural/oral. (2) including 'extensive' reading. (3) using graded tests.
(4) by using, for example, newspaper articles, including literary and artistic criticisms.

Thus it can be seen that in the initial stages structures should occupy most of the teacher's time, but then progressively this emphasis should decrease.

At the upper secondary stage, since it is assumed that the basic mechanisms of the language are known, linguistically the emphasis must be upon the extension of vocabulary, the study of written as opposed to oral structures, and the achievement of complete oral fluency. Naturally a 'care and maintenance' task must be undertaken of all that has been previously taught. But this is also the stage at which the pupil should begin to gain real benefit from his knowledge of the language by extending his horizons to include the complete culture of the linguistic area that he is studying. To a certain extent this is an unachievable ideal, largely because of the exigencies of the terminal examination. How far this study may be taken is also dependent on the number of hours available. Figures for these have already been given, but a further comparison between West Germany and England is interesting. In West Germany, although English is the first foreign language studied in the *Gymnasium*, less time is devoted to it in the terminal stages of secondary education than to French—a fact which is explained in terms of the greater time spent on English lower down in school. However, a pupil studying both English and French in the last two years of the *Gymnasium* course will spend some 570 hours upon them; in England, although figures vary considerably, a pupil taking French and German for G.C.E. 'A' Level will, in his last two years, spend some 600 hours upon those subjects. Yet, whereas the German pupil in the terminal examination—the *Abitur*—will also be examined in religion, German, social studies, mathematics, art or music, one science, and physical education, it is highly unlikely that the English pupil will be *examined* in more than one other subject, and this is usually one of the humanities. In the West German context the *Gymnasium* pupil studying two languages, as well as a number of other subjects, as has been seen, is held to be 'specializing' in languages, but there is clearly no comparison with the specialization or study in depth that the pupil in England undergoes. Perhaps it would be more exact to describe the German system as one in which a particular 'bias' is given to the course. It is noteworthy that only in about half the countries in Western Europe is it possible to 'specialize' in either sense of the term in modern languages.

Differences regarding three particular facets of language teaching —pronunciation, grammar, and vocabulary—should be mentioned.

In pronunciation practice the use of phonetics and familiarity with the phonetic script has considerably declined over the past decade, even for the recognition of phonemes. This is largely because of the wider currency of audio-visual aids of all kinds. In Denmark, however, Jespersen's script is still widely used. There is not much evidence as yet that phonetic linguistics has spread to the classroom level, so that systematic comparisons of phonemes in the source and target languages are still not usually made. Everywhere the tendency is to give priority to oral fluency rather than to grammatical accuracy, on the grounds that this is a more 'natural' way of learning a foreign language analogous to the way in which one learnt the mother tongue. Oral exercises are many and varied: the use of 'situations', renarration (the oral reproduction of a text previously studied), summarizing orally a text, making reports, describing experiences, dramatizing texts, making speeches and giving talks, participation in discussions and debates, learning by heart of prose and poetry, and even extempore interpreting.

In *grammar* the stress is on the functional rather than the formal. With beginners this often merely takes the form of memorized dialogues, which are developed from real-life situations and have inter-substitutable parts. Drills and pattern practice, instead of consisting of isolated examples, are usually contextualized, realistic, and varied, and so far as possible linked with each other in a meaningful sequence. The distinction is also drawn between the productive (active) and the receptive (passive) knowledge of functional grammar.

As regards *vocabulary*, the use of word-lists is discreet. For English, reference is still made in some countries to Michael West's *General Service List*, but other lists are also used—in Germany, for example, the *Grund- und Aufbauwortschatz: Englisch* (Klett-Verlag). There is a well-grounded fear that a slavish adherence to word-lists may, however, adversely affect method. Passages based exclusively on such lists might become monotonous or appear unimaginative because of the need to exclude certain words. Motivation of the pupil is of primary importance. It is generally agreed that effective vocabulary learning can occur only through contextualization, careful grading, and so far as possible the avoidance of translation, particularly if a lexical item is taught for productive use. At a recent conference it was considered that the first three years of language learning were a stage in which the control of vocabulary and its division into productive (active) and receptive (passive) use was all-important, and that word-lists based on frequency counts with appropriate situational vocabulary were vital checks for the teacher. This control, however, did not mean that pupils should not learn 'international' words or 'loan' words, or words similar in form or meaning to the mother tongue.

Most countries do not specify in their official directives details of the vocabulary to be acquired. Belgium, for example, merely states that in the first two years about 500 words of English should be known. In Norway a word-list of about 2000 words has been published to cover the first five years of learning a language. Germany by the end of its nine-year *Gymnasium* course expects the pupil to know some 3000 to 4000 words for productive use. In France, in the first four years of secondary education, it is stated that the rate of vocabulary acquisition should not exceed 600 to 700 words a year. In England it is usually reckoned that to pass O Level French a pupil needs to know some 1500 to 2000 words, but to pass in German some 2000 to 2500. It has been estimated that the average Englishman hardly ever uses more than 2000 words in his productive vocabulary, and yet Webster's *New International Dictionary* contains over 450,000 lexical items. It is obvious that for learners whose native language contains few words of Romance or Greek origin English vocabulary must prove exceptionally difficult. It was Jespersen who once remarked that about half of the English language was "undemocratic", by which he meant that it was composed of words of this kind.(7)

The exercise of translation is at the moment the black sheep of the European modern languages reforming 'establishment'—probably rightly so, not because it is harmful in itself, but because as an examination exercise it impinges harmfully upon teaching. More will be said of its role in examinations later. Yet it stubbornly survives all attempts to oust it, at least at pre-university level. It is perhaps noteworthy, however, that in Sweden no translation is allowed in school, and none even at university level for the intending modern-languages teacher. Even although translation has been unqualifiedly condemned, there are nevertheless influential groups, particularly in institutions of higher education, which cling to the view that translation, whether from source language into target language or *vice versa*, remains one of the supreme tests of command of a foreign language. On the other hand, it is not an exercise that appeals greatly to the average pupil, who feels that in a real-life situation it is not an accomplishment that he will often need. Perhaps for it could be substituted interpreting exercises, which may have real practical value and at the same time, since they are oral, might motivate the best modern-language pupils more. If such exercises were practised the teacher would have at first to accept very crude approximations to what the speaker in the native language was really saying, which would then become increasingly sophisticated as linguistic competence grew. A variant of this might be translation from the target language into the source language, which is, of course, a far easier task. A further variant might consist in a pupil reacting in the foreign language to a statement made by another speaker in a meaningful situation. Such a dialogue could be stimulated by the preparation beforehand of the set of statements to be made by Speaker A. There are, of course, occasions when translation becomes indispensable. Many European countries use it, for example, as a quick means of verifying whether some particular element of the foreign language has been understood.

The whole field of ancillary aids has blossomed enormously during the past decade. Furthermore, their use is left much more to the discretion of the teacher. This is even so with such a conventional aid as the textbook. In many countries, such as France, Iceland, Italy, the Netherlands, Switzerland, and the United Kingdom, within very broad limits, the teacher has a completely free choice in selecting the books he will use, although usually prescribed texts—if any exist—are laid down for the secondary leaving examination. In Austria, Denmark, Finland, West Germany, Norway, Spain, and Sweden the teacher enjoys a limited right of choice, usually from a list of books approved or recommended by the central education authorities. Only in three countries—Cyprus, Greece, and Luxembourg—are the books prescribed by the central education authorities. In the present state of the textbook market there is much to be said in any case for some 'vetting' of textbooks before they are used in schools. The abundance of choice is often a positive hindrance to the young and inexperienced teacher, or, for that matter, to the experienced one, who cannot possibly know the whole range of the market.

It is, however, in the use of educational technology for language teaching that the real breakthrough in ancillary aids has occurred. Teaching foreign languages by radio is universal—the success in West Germany of the B.B.C.'s English programme *Walter and Connie* was phenomenal. As yet television has been little exploited outside the larger countries. In the installation of language laboratories Sweden, West Germany, France, Belgium, and Britain have taken the lead. In Finland, Norway, and Switzerland the number of laboratories is increasing, but in Austria, Greece, Italy, Netherlands, Spain, and Turkey they are still comparatively few. Although the use of the tape-recorder is universally accepted, language laboratories as such still have their critics. It is said that their rationale is based essentially upon a behaviourist view of language: the inculcation of automatisms, which are practised in the laboratory to the point of saturation and sometimes to the point of boredom. The unwisdom of increasing learning practice to the level of tedium, which might produce a negative feedback, is apparent. The critics claim also that the isolation of the laboratory environment, despite its great advantages in overcoming selfconsciousness, may also produce a negative attitude. A development based upon the language laboratory is that of a language workshop where the pupil may either use individual aids to learning or work in a group with the help of a number of technological resources; this is now being actively considered in many European countries. The workshop allows for the use simultaneously of a number of different aids, according to pupil and teacher need. Whereas the thirty-two-booth language laboratory costs about £7000, the alternative resources required in a language workshop, such as audio-active cassette laboratory tape-recorders, conventional tape-recorders, projectors, a video-tape-recorder, and a loop projector, together with appropriate reprographic material, might well cost under £2000. Certainly the workshop gives greater flexibility in teaching approach, permitting individualization of learning as well as work in small groups.

There is no doubt that the use of educational technology in language learning will continue to increase as more sophisticated hardware is developed. In the first flush of enthusiasm it was even hoped that it might reduce the number of language teachers required. This is now seen not to be the case. What it may well do is to increase immeasurably the efficiency of language teaching and learning.(8)

CHAPTER 5—NOTES

(1) Adapted from R. Poignant, *L'enseignement dans les pays du marché commun* (Paris, 1965), Table 10, p. 67.

(2) R. Titone, "La preparazione dei manuali moderni per l'insegnamento delle lingue stramiere: criteri didattici", *Orientamenti Pedagogici*, Anno IX, No. 4, 1962, p. 666.

(3) Mr Breitenstein, Dutch delegate to the joint British Council/Council of Europe Conference on Curricula for the Teaching of English in European Secondary Schools, held in London in May 1969.

(4) Abstracted from a background paper presented by S. Johannson to a British Council/Council of Europe conference held in London in May 1969.

(5) M. Lemaire, "L'enseignement de la seconde langue (II)", *Bulletin d'Information* (Bruxelles, No. 4, April 1968).

(6) M. Lemaire *et al.*, "La seconde langue dans l'enseignement du vocabulaire", *Bulletin d'Information* (Bruxelles, No. 5, May 1968).

(7) A. Chamberlin, *Learning a Passive Vocabulary*, p. 29.

(8) I am indebted to the English-Teaching Information Centre (ETIC) for information contained in annual reports of the International Conference on Second Language Problems, and also for information contained in the Background Papers prepared by ETIC for the joint British Council/Council of Europe Conference on Curricula for the Teaching of English in European Secondary Schools, held in London in May 1969.

Chapter 6
Examinations in Modern Languages

The gamut of possible examinations at the end of secondary education which exists in England—C.S.E., G.C.E. O Level, G.C.E. A Level, G.C.E. Special Papers, the Oxbridge Scholarship Examinations, with the possibility or threat of an I Level, to be situated at an intermediate stage between O and A Level, must certainly make the English system of secondary education the most over-examined in the world. Certainly no other country in Western Europe examines so religiously its potential entrants to higher education. Most countries content themselves with one final examination, such as the *baccalauréat*, the *Abitur*, or the *certificat de fin d'études* in France, West Germany, and Belgium respectively. Furthermore, because of the lack of specialization in the terminal phase of upper secondary education the final examination in modern languages on the Continent is much less involved than the English G.C.E. examinations. (Table 11 shows the other subjects studied in the terminal phase of secondary education in the various countries by those pupils whose main speciality is modern languages.)

The main function of examinations in modern languages must be either to serve as a stimulant to the pupil to redouble his efforts or to evaluate the progress that he has made. Furthermore, in connection with entrance to higher education, such examinations must also have some predictive validity and act as a prognosis of future success. There is no doubt that examinations at this level do act as an incentive to both teacher and pupil, although in certain cases they may also prove to be a *disincentive*. In the traditional sense they are also recognized to set the seal upon secondary education and to open the door to post-secondary education. Yet everywhere the conventional system of examinations is being called into question. Only recently has the relationship between the aims and objectives of teaching modern languages and their evaluation been fully recognized. A primordial condition for the validity of any examination must surely

Table 11—Other subjects studied in terminal stage by pupils whose main speciality is modern languages

Subjects	Dk	Ge(1)	Fi	Fr	Lux G.(8)	Lux B.(16)	Ma	Sd
					Countries			
1. Mother tongue	×	×	×	×			×	×
2. Religion	×	×	×		×(9)	×(9)	×	×
3. Philosophy		×(2)		×			×/	×
4. Politics								
5. Civics	×			(7)	×(10)	×(10)	×/	×
6. History	×		×	(7)	×(11)	×(11)	(×)	
7. Geography			(5)	(7)			(×)	
8. History, Geography, and Civics				×				
9. Economics and Social Studies								
10. Art		×/(3)	×	(×)	×	(×)	(×)	×(19)
11. Music	×	×/(3)		(×)	×		(×)	×
12. Latin	×					×	(×)	
13. Greek				×/				
14. Latin and Greek Literature in translation	×(18)							
15. Greek authors								
16. Domestic Science					×(12)	×	(×`)	
17. Child-minding					×(13)			
18. Psychology			×					×
19. Biology	×		(5)					
20. Chemistry		×/(4)			×(14)	×(17)		}×(20)
21. Physics		×/(4)			×(15)	×(17)		
22. Geology and Geography		×/(4)	×					
23. Physical Sciences				×	×	×		
24. Mathematics	×	×	×	(×)	×			×
25. Crafts			×(6)					×
26. P.E.	×	×		×	×	×		×

General notes

/—there is a choice between two or more subjects, one of which must be taken.
( )—entirely optional.

Belgium has a modern-language speciality in the technical schools.

The following have no modern-language speciality: Cyprus, Ireland, Italy, Spain, and Turkey.

No relevant information on courses stressing modern languages is available for the Netherlands, which does not have a modern-language speciality as such: English, French, and German are all obligatory throughout. More time is given to languages in the economics branch. There is a set syllabus for all pupils. This will be changed in about five years' time—*i.e.*, about 1975, when specialization will be possible.

In the United Kingdom pupils following an Arts course may in the penultimate and final years (sixth form) take two, or even three, languages to A Level. They may also study about two or three other subjects, usually arts subjects, along with these. There are no obligatory subjects. In the pre-penultimate year the syllabus is less specialized. Here, too, a pupil may take two modern languages and a combination of about six other subjects, usually including English language.

Notes

(1) Refers to *Hessen*.

(2) *Gemeinschaftskunde*.

(3) Art or Music.

(4) Physics or Chemistry or Biology.

(5) See subject No. 22.

(6) Physical Education and Hygienics.

(7) See subject No. 8.

(8) *Enseignement secondaire pour jeunes filles*.

(9) Christian doctrine.

(10) *Droit publique et administratif*.

(11) General and national History.

(12) *Branches ménagères sociales, artistiques (ordre ménager)*.

(13) *Puériculture*.

(14) Includes an optional half-hour per week of practical work.

(15) Does not seem to include any practical work.

(16) *Enseignement secondaire pour garçons—enseignement classique*.

(17) Does not include any practical work.

(18) Classical civilization.

(19) Art or Music are alternatives; history of Art is also studied.

(20) 'Natural Sciences'.

be prior agreement between teachers and examiners as to what is required to be evaluated. Under the old dispensation, where examiners were often felt to be super-inspectors, the teacher learnt what the examiner was looking for in candidates by reflecting on his own schooldays, when he had himself sat for similar examinations, and by the bitter experience of his pupils' failure. There was thus an implicit process of arbitration going on between teacher and examiner in which the examiner laid down the rules. The first condition for a clearer concept of language examinations is therefore for clear indications to be given by teachers to examiners as to what has been taught, and by examiners to teachers as to what they intend to examine. This may be a truism, but in the European context it is one that has in the past been too often neglected.

In Western Europe, therefore, the present concern of language examinations—as indeed of examinations in other subjects—is with reliability and validity. The difficulties of tackling the problem of reliability for written expression in the foreign language are over-whelming, particularly if the conventional essay-type question is the rule. The problems of validity are no less formidable. In languages it is extremely difficult to deal with the question of content validity —to produce a linguistically valid test—simply because what should be the precise content of a language course leading to a terminal examination has not yet been delineated in sufficient detail. If one looks for concurrent validity also the problems are immense. The most obvious norm with which to compare examination results must be the teachers' estimates, or at least performance in class-work. These are in fact taken into account in West Germany, for example. (But one Secretary of a large English examining board informed the present writer that teachers' estimates were in fact "never looked at".) Yet another form of validity is construct validity. Davies(1) has defined this as what the examination in languages means in terms of a psychological construct, and goes on to ask what the pupil in the end must be able to *do*. What in fact should be the *terminal behaviour* aimed at? He declares that it must be the ability to handle certain 'situations' in the foreign language. Again, these 'situations' must be very exactly elaborated. But since we are dealing with the end of secondary education, the most difficult norm to achieve is that of predictive validity: how well will the pupil perform in any continuing form of post-secondary education? It is now realized practically everywhere in Europe that conventional essay-type questions con-centrated over a few days no longer suffice, and other methods of assessment must be experimented with. Although in England few examining boards have yet introduced objective-type testing, these tests, particularly of the multiple-choice type, are being used in-creasingly in Europe, especially in Sweden. Although this kind of testing comes closest to complying with the criteria of reliability and validity that are required, the critics assert that such tests cannot measure the creative manipulation of the foreign language, which is the hall-mark of being able to use it effectively. Perhaps a develop-ment for the future may be Computer Assisted Learning (CAL) in which assessment will be built in the learning process. In the U.S.A. attempts to teach the grammatical aspects of foreign languages by this means are already under way. In CAL the pupil carries out the task assigned to him in the foreign language programme, which is then verified by the computer. According to the level of achievement, the next task for the pupil will be assigned according to computerized data. Thus the process will be one of individualization as well as of built-in continuous evaluation. The French are experimenting with the concept of the *examen-bilan* (the 'balance-sheet' approach) which would assess the pupil on the basis of his overall achievement. Such achievement would be calculated according to the marks obtained in any written examination or test, the teachers' estimates and school record, and his rating in an oral examination. The 'weighting' of these independent variables could vary according to whether the dependent variable was the prediction of language competence in higher education, the prediction of success in industrial or business training courses, or, for that matter, in a professional interpreter's course. It is plainly nonsensical to 'weight' independent variables in the same way for all purposes, no matter how these are spelled out. On the other hand, for the examination terminating academic secondary education a fixed 'weighting' in terms of the skills and competences required may be acceptable. Such a matrix, in the form of an analysis of the percentage mark distribution, was approved by a group of European experts meeting under the joint aegis of the Council of Europe and the Italian Government at Ostia in spring 1966. The analysis is given below:

Analysis of Percentage Mark Distribution

Elements of Syllabus (general examples only)	Comprehension		Expression		Scope for spontaneous or original expression in the foreign language
	Listening	Reading	Speaking	Writing	
Comprehension —Listening	20	+			
Comprehension —Reading		20			
Composition				30	+
Oral tests	+	+	30		+
Totals	20+	20++	30	30	++

Notes

+—indicates a secondary function.

Distribution between comprehension and expression ('receptive' and 'productive' aspects) of 40 per cent and 60 per cent respectively.

Moreover, as between aural/oral elements (Listening and Speaking) and reading/writing elements (Reading and Writing) distribution is 50 per cent each.

How good in fact have we been up to now in making an accurate prognosis? Does school performance in foreign languages at present act as an accurate predictor for success in university studies in languages? A study of this was made by Marklund, Henrysson, and Paulin.(2) The study considered a number of international investigations. The mean of the various validity coefficients referring to prediction of academic success for languages showed a correlation coefficient of 0·31 between marks in foreign languages at school and university success in languages. Such a correlation is not particularly high, but it must be remembered that the language population in question was, by definition, highly selective, and this would lower the correlation.

If the French are moving towards the concept of the 'balance-sheet' form of examination, the Swedes have adopted a system of continuous assessment. This is carried out in the last two years of the *gymnasiet* (which is the three-year upper academic school for the 16–19 age group, corresponding to the *Oberstufe* of the German *Gymnasium*, the three-year course in the French *lycée*, or an English sixth form). Assessment takes place in part by means of standardized achievement tests, which are elaborated by the National Board of Education, and are spread over the period each year from November to May. In languages the tests given are of the objective type. A panel of up to ten experts in the languages concerned, with the help of two psychologists, is responsible for making an analysis of the objectives of language teaching at this level and for the overall framework of the test. Another group of experts then takes over and actually writes the test items. Pre-testing of items takes place on a representative sample of pupils. In the light of the results of the pre-testing the final test is elaborated, and this is then taken in the *gymnasiet*. Upon the basis of the results norms are established for the whole country. After the teacher of the individual class has been informed of what the norms are for the particular test he then calculates the distribution and mean for his own class. The Swedish Education Act of 1964 concerning the *gymnasiet* lays down that marks should be awarded on a five-point scale, with three as the mean. Thus the mark for all pupils in the same grade taking a foreign language should be distributed according to a normal distribution approximately as follows:

Mark	1	2	3	4	5
Percentage of candidates	7	24	38	24	7

It must be emphasized, however, that the norms of the tests received by the teacher are not the only basis upon which he may calculate the final mark in languages for each of his pupils. Before a final mark is awarded the teacher makes a preliminary assessment based on his own judgment and on continuous assessment throughout the school term. He then calculates the distribution and mean for his *own* marks and compares them with the test results. In this way the teacher can see how his own pupils compare with other pupils on a nationwide basis. Thus, if there are discrepancies between the two distributions and the two means, the teacher is advised to adjust his own marks as closely as possible to the test distribution. In making the adjustment of his preliminary marks the teacher should rank his pupils according to their overall achievement. It must be noted, however, that the teacher has always the final say in deciding exactly what mark should be awarded for each pupil.

It is over the nature of the tests that there is likely to be the most controversy. They are all standardized achievement tests, mainly of the objective type, with multiple-choice answers. The objections to this kind of test are numerous. It is argued that selection of the correct answer from four or five alternatives leads to a certain passivity in learning because inevitably the form of testing has a retroactive effect on the teaching process. The opponent of the conventional essay-type question may argue that a similar adverse 'backwash' exists with this kind of question also. But it is asserted also that objective tests cannot test a candidate's ability to reason and argue effectively in the foreign language, nor his capacity to manipulate the language creatively. (This argument is obviously analogous to that adduced against audio-visual courses, where it is alleged that only stimulus-response automatisms can be induced in the learner, and that the main task—the ability to react spontaneously and creatively in a linguistic situation—has still to be tackled once the groundwork of 'stamped-in' patterns and structures has been covered.) On the other hand, for the testing of pure knowledge, whether of grammar and structures or of culture and literature, as distinct from the *application* of knowledge, there would seem to be little valid argument against objective tests.

Objective tests for foreign languages are widely used in North America. A typical battery of tests is that compiled by the Modern Languages Association of America, and consists of the following:

(a) *Listening comprehension tests:*
1. *Rejoinders* to be made to statements heard on a tape. The appropriate one has to be selected.
2. *Simple dialogue:* the candidate has to choose the correct statement to be made by speaker B in response to speaker A.
3. *Answering questions on a text:* the candidate listens to a text and then has to answer a number of questions upon it, choosing his answers from a number of alternatives.

65

(b) *Speaking tests:*
1. *Repetition* of sentences.
2. *Description* of pictorial material—*e.g.*, a candidate might be given an imaginary street-plan and be asked to direct someone from point A to B by the shortest route.

(c) *Reading tests:*
1. *Incomplete statements:* the correct phrase has to be selected in order to complete a statement appropriately.
2. *Reading passage:* alternatives have to be given for certain words.

(d) *Writing tests:*
1. *Incomplete context:* blanks in a connected passage in the foreign language have to be filled in correctly so that they make sense.
2. *Inter-linear exercise:* appropriate corrections have to be made to a passage containing a number of errors which have to be distinguished by the candidate.

(e) *Civilization and culture tests:* these usually consist of a number of multiple-choice 'general knowledge' items.

Many of these tests can be of the multiple-choice type, but not necessarily so. What they have in common is that they are comparatively easy to mark, and, within their limitations, have measurable reliability and validity. As yet in Europe only Sweden has adopted them unreservedly, although similar exercises have been tried out in England at G.C.E. O Level. Other countries are also experimenting with them because of the influx of numbers of candidates in languages, and because of their undoubted advantages in objectivity. But it is doubtful whether this kind of test will ever supplant completely the traditional kind of European languages examination—but it may well supplement it. To these traditional examinations we must now turn.

A summary of the content of the written examination in modern languages which terminates secondary education is given for a number of countries in Table 12 below. From it can be seen that despite the almost universal condemnation of translation by European experts, both as a teaching method and as an examination technique at school level, it surprisingly survives in over half the countries of Western Europe as an examination exercise. In fairness it must be said that several countries state categorically that they intend to abolish it. Translation into the mother tongue is far more

Table 12—The terminal examination in modern languages: summary of written examination

	Bg	Cy	Dk(5)	Ge	Fi	Fr	Ir	It	Ma	Lux	Neth	Sp	Tu(2)	UK (E)
Translation														
1. From mother tongue	Yes(1)	No	Yes	No	Yes	No	Yes	Yes	Yes(3)	No	No	No	No	Yes
2. Into mother tongue	Yes(1)	No	No	No	Yes	Yes	Yes	No	Yes(3)	No	Yes	Yes	Yes	Yes
3. Use of dictionary	No	n.a.*	No	n.a.	No	No	No	Yes	No	n.a.	No	Yes	No	No
Free Composition	Yes	Yes	No	Yes(2)	Yes	No	Yes	No	Yes	Yes	Yes(4)	No	No	Yes
Questions on literature and civilization	Yes	No	No	No	No	No	Yes	No	Yes	Yes(2)	Yes	No	No	Yes
Explication de texte	No	No	Yes	Yes(2)	No	Yes	No	No	Yes	No	No	No	No	No
Reproduction	Yes	Yes	Yes	Yes(6)	No	No	No	No	No	No	No	No	No	No
Dictation	No	No	No	No	No	No	No	Yes(2)	Yes	No	No	No	Yes	Yes

Notes

(1) "no fixed rule".

(2) Not frequently/only occasionally. For translation from mother tongue, Turkey said "rarely"—and then only one or two sentences.

(3) To and from English (*not* Maltese).

(4) Only in school type—HBS-A.

(5) The teacher may set a précis. The original text may be in English or Danish.

(6) Mostly with commentary.

* n.a.—not applicable.

usual than translation into the target language as an examination exercise, although several countries—Finland, Ireland, and the United Kingdom, for example—expect candidates to be able to translate both ways. In England the reform of A Level so as to do away with translation completely has been mooted since 1964, and even earlier. That no developments have occurred since is due in part to the lack of a central authority to legislate upon such matters, and also to the strong hold that university teachers of modern languages in England have upon the modern-language syllabuses at school level. These university teachers hold that translation is the most effective instrument for testing whether a candidate has a really effective mastery of the foreign language. Unfortunately, in order to select with maximum accuracy the comparatively few who specialize in modern languages at the university, they impose this exercise with its injurious effect upon teaching method even upon those who have no intention of specializing in this way. The Ostia conference, following Vietor's dictum of some seventy-five years earlier, had considered that translation "should only be introduced at university level". Incidentally, Spain and Italy seem to be the only two countries that allow the use of the dictionary in the examination room. This in itself is significant. If an examination is to simulate a real-life situation, then surely the use of such reference works should be allowed. The engineer designing a bridge is granted access to any reference data that he may require; even the poet is not denied a rhyming dictionary!

Free composition and *explication de texte* are usually alternatives in the final examination. West Germany has no fixed rule and may use either as a testing technique. But Italy, Spain, and Turkey use neither of these two forms in their examination. Renarration (or reproduction) is used as an examination technique only in Belgium, Cyprus, Denmark, and West Germany. Dictation forms part of the examination in the United Kingdom and Malta, which in this respect follows British practice, but is also occasionally used in Italy and Turkey.

Only about half the countries of Western Europe set questions on foreign literature and civilization, although, as has been seen, both the literature and the culture of the foreign country or countries are studied almost everywhere. It must be admitted that other countries in Western Europe consider ludicrous the English system of examining literature at this level. The idea of answering questions on the foreign literature in the mother tongue conflicts totally with the principles to which all countries nominally subscribe, namely of teaching (and therefore of examining) through the medium of the foreign language. The English practice can only be assumed to be due to the survival of practices associated with the classical languages, when questions concerning history or literature were naturally answered in English. The practice is also due, in part, to the exigencies of the English universities who, unlike their Continental counterparts, still rarely give lectures in the foreign language and whose degree examinations also contain, for example, questions on French literature that must be answered in English.

Although the discussion of examinations has mainly concerned the terminal examination, it should be mentioned that there has been comparative neglect of the use of evaluation techniques as diagnostic instruments. Without going to extreme lengths it is valuable for both teacher and pupil to learn just how well a particular language skill has been mastered and, what is more, retained over a period of time. Graded tests, internationally standardized, might well be elaborated for particular facets of English.

A further useful development that might be envisaged is the production of general standardized international tests of linguistic attainment for the main European languages. These might have great practical utility. Progress towards equivalences has already made such strides that young people are proceeding more than ever to study in higher education abroad. Thus, for example, young Turks go to study engineering at the University of Vienna. They may well arrive without a sufficient knowledge of the German language, in which case they have to take 'crash' language courses. It would obviously be advantageous if, before moving to Austria, the Turkish student could take an examination in German which would be internationally recognized as enabling him to follow lectures and courses in German.

There are at present about 600,000 students studying at universities in countries other than their own, and about one-third of these are located in the United States. It is also estimated that about one-third of these students arriving in the United States do in fact require additional English instruction in order to participate fully in university courses. To deal in part with this problem a special Test of English as a Foreign Language (TOEFL) was devised. This is a 270-item objective test lasting some three hours and consisting of some five sub-tests. It is widely used as a grading device for deficiencies in English by American universities. Since student mobility is likely to increase in Western Europe also, it would seem advisable that similar tests to TOEFL should be established, at least in English, French, and German. Internationally recognized, these tests could be administered in the countries from which the students originate and their standards accepted in the 'host' countries.

In order to give some idea of the present structure of the terminal

69

examinations in languages in upper academic secondary education, case studies are given of Belgium, France, and West Germany.

A. *BELGIUM*

The Belgian terminal examination is in two parts, held at Christmas and in June. All subjects are examined at an oral examination at Christmas. The final examination in the terminal class in June is written.

As regards the written examination in modern languages, there are no fixed rules. A reform proposed by the teachers envisages the following divisions:

> *Written:*
> Reading comprehension 15 per cent
> Aural comprehension 15
> Essay-writing 30
>
> *Oral:*
> (*a*) Free exposition by candidate
> (*b*) Conversation on unprepared subject-matter
> (*c*) Questions on prepared subject-matter 40
>
> ———
>
> 100 per cent

At present there is no fixed rule regarding *translation* as an examination exercise. Where it is set, dictionaries may not be used. If *free composition* is given the teacher is responsible for setting the topics —three in all, which may be general, literary, or scientific in nature. The candidate may choose two, and is expected to devote fifty minutes to each. Again, the use of a dictionary is not permitted. The mode of assessment differs considerably according to the teacher who corrects them. Questions may also be set on *literature and civilization*, but again there is no fixed rule.

In any case, there is a list of recommended authors published in the official Ministry programmes. Up to now these texts have been mainly of a literary nature, but there is some reaction against this tendency. They have also been mainly concerned with literature from the Romantic period up to modern times, but this is very flexible. The study of extracts is permitted. Either in the oral or in the written examination the teacher has the duty to verify that the texts have in fact been read. In any case, all questions on literature must be answered in the foreign language. Teachers are fairly free to choose what means they feel appropriate for the pupils to acquire a knowledge of the literature and civilization of the foreign country, but in practice, of course, the choice must be limited by the availability of books and manuals.

Textual commentary as an examination exercise is generally not used, although this is regretted. Nor is *reproduction* used. *Dictation* as an examination exercise is used mainly in the lower classes and not in the terminal examination.

Up to now the *oral examination* has been chiefly used as an instrument for the verification of subject-matter. The reform under way aims at assessing the ability for personal expression. Likewise it is hoped to effect a change, so that the oral examinations test different capacities in the future from the written examinations. To some extent there is a guarantee that all qualities will be assessed, because the examiner is the candidate's own teacher. The examiner is also allowed at the oral to probe weaknesses that may have revealed themselves during the written examination. He may or may not be assisted by a colleague in this. Candidates are interrogated on their personal reading and on a text that they have prepared in advance (this for the *examen de maturité* only). The examination lasts about a quarter of an hour and candidates are tested individually. The candidate may be asked to read a text aloud—sometimes a passage already done in class. If the text is unseen, however, the candidate prepares it in advance, must make an oral résumé, comment on it, and reply to the examiner's questions. One innovation that may be introduced is the use of pictures upon the basis of which the candidate must tell a story. Sometimes the oral discussion may turn upon contemporary problems. At present general conversation does not figure in the oral examination, but may well do so if the reform is carried through.

No marking scheme for the oral examination is prescribed, although in practice most examiners have a detailed scheme in mind, rather than working solely upon 'global' impressions, and allot marks for different linguistic or 'content' aspects of the examination.

It must be remembered that the oral examination takes place at Christmas in the final year, and not in June. The *examen de maturité* (university-entrance examination) does take place, however, at the end of the terminal year. For this the pupil must present orally one or two subjects of his own choice. If one of those subjects is a foreign language he is given the choice of one of three texts that are unseen. He reads it, prepares a résumé and a commentary, and then presents these exercises orally to the examiners, who may question him and extend the scope of the questions to other fields.

Up to now there have been no tests of reading comprehension or of aural comprehension, but, as noted above, these are proposed in the present reforms.

The marking of written papers is the responsibility of the class teacher, who need not work to any marking scheme. There is no formal control of the marking, but inspectors may occasionally intervene. Candidates failing the examination may present themselves at a second examination session in September; failure a second time entails repeating the year. In evaluating a candidate class-work in the last year and the results of the Christmas examination count for half the total marks.

It would appear that in Belgium the greatest possible freedom is given to the teacher in evaluating his pupils.

B. *FRANCE*

In France the main concentration on languages occurs in the Philosophy-Letters section, in sub-sections A2, A4, and A5, in all of which are *written papers*. There is set a passage for *guided commentary* of some thirty lines in length, for which, out of a total of twenty, fourteen marks are awarded, and a *translation* from the foreign language into French, of some ten to twelve lines, for which six marks are awarded. The written examination lasts in all three hours.

For the *guided commentary* the following instructions are given to those setting the texts:

> Simple, well-thought-out questions will guide, will 'direct' the efforts of the candidates. They will assist them in bringing out the general meaning of the text or its most important aspects, in discovering the sequence and linkage of ideas, in expounding a situation, in analysing a character, etc. It would not appear in the interest of the candidate to reduce the number of questions unduly. The setter of the subject will decide upon this number depending upon the length to which they might be developed, without, however, in principle, going beyond five or six. It would clearly be fortunate if there were between them an organic link which would allow the candidates to reply in the form of a sequential exposition. (It is also recalled that there should be chosen only) texts taken from authors of high quality, immediately clear to native contemporary readers of the language, fully intelligible by themselves without the need of a special documentation.

A further instruction says that rare words and difficult expressions must be explained or translated as footnotes. (Two recent texts from the French *baccalauréat* are given as an annexe to this case-study.) The guided commentary consists of a discussion of the content, an analysis of the composition of the passage, and of remarks on the style, etc. There are no questions relating to external criticism or presupposing knowledge of literary history or history of civilization.

The *translation* into French consists of some lines taken from the piece set for guided commentary, and it is expected that candidates shall devote one third of the examination time to this. It is usually descriptive, narrative, or may be an extract from an essay.

Guided commentary and translation into French constitute the only forms of exercise proposed at the written examination. Between the written and the *oral examination* there is no essential difference, apart from the obvious fact that one tests written, the other verbal expression. The oral has as its aim the evaluation of mastery of the spoken language and ability to understand a text. The examination consists of the reading of a passage already studied during the school year, followed by a discussion upon it in the foreign language, with occasionally the translation of a few lines of the text. Candidates are examined individually, and not as a group, by one examiner only, and no tape-recordings are made of the oral examination. The examiner may, if he so desires, know already how the candidate has fared in the written examination. Since the passage set for the candidate must be from works studied during the year—a list of which is appended to the candidate's school record—the questions at the oral are not prepared in advance. The candidate has approximately a quarter of an hour to prepare, and the examination itself lasts as long. Since the teacher can choose his own texts for study in class, there is no list of set authors or books as such, although the manual from which the teacher makes his choice has had, of course, to be approved by the authorities. Usually the examination is limited to what has been described, and there is no general discussion of other topics.

The assessment of the oral is in principle a 'global' one, with a final mark out of twenty, but individual examiners are free to make what sub-divisions they like in order to arrive at a final mark.

Neither *reading comprehension* nor *aural comprehension* forms part of the oral examination.

Modern-language examiners are drawn from secondary teachers, but these may not teach in the school from which a candidate is drawn. There is no external control of their marking. The failure in one subject, such as modern languages, does not necessarily mean that the candidate will have failed the whole *baccalauréat*, which depends on the total marks arrived at in all subjects.

The French system of examining in modern languages seems characterized by comparative simplicity, with the candidate's reaction to a text and ability to translate into French as the instruments whereby linguistic competence can be judged.

Sample examination papers for 1968 are given below:

ANGLAIS

Texte

The Importance of Tradition

What enables men to know more than their ancestors is that they start with a knowledge of what their ancestors have already learned. They are able to do advanced experiments which increase knowledge because they do not have to repeat the elementary experiments. It is tradition which brings them to the point where advanced experimentation is possible. This is the meaning of tradition. This is why a society can be progressive only if it conserves its tradition.

The notion that every problem can be studied as such with an open and empty mind, without preconception,[1] without already knowing what has already been learned about it, must condemn men to a chronic childishness. For no man, and no generation of men, is capable of inventing for itself the arts and sciences of a high civilization. No-one, and no one generation, is capable of rediscovering all the truths men need, of developing sufficient knowledge by applying a mere intelligence, no matter how acute, to mere observation, no matter how accurate. The men of any generation, as Bernard of Chartres put it, are like dwarfs seated on the shoulders of giants. If we are to "see more things than the ancients and things more distinct" it is "due neither to the sharpness of our sight nor the greatness of our stature", but "simply because they have lent us their own".

For individuals do not have the time, the opportunity, or the energy to make all the experiments and to discern all the significance that have gone into the making of the whole heritage of civilization. In developing knowledge men must collaborate with their ancestors. Otherwise they must begin, not where their ancestors arrived, but where their ancestors began. If they exclude the tradition of the past from the curricula of the schools they make it necessary for each generation to repeat the errors rather than benefit by the successes of its predecessors.

WALTER LIPPMANN, "Education versus Western
Civilization"
The American Scholar, Spring 1941.

Travail à faire par le candidat

I. COMMENTAIRE DIRIGÉ (sur 14 points)

1. Sum up what the word 'tradition' means in this passage.
2. What do you think of the comparison: "like dwarfs seated on the shoulders of giants"?

[1] *preconception*—an opinion formed in advance.

3. Which is more important in the history of science and invention: tradition or the individual achievements of men of genius?
4. Isn't there another sense of the word 'tradition'?
    Show how tradition may become a burden (*un fardeau*).
    Find examples in everyday life, and in the study of English or French civilization.

II. VERSION (sur 6 points)

Translate into French from "The notion that every problem . . ." to ". . . the shoulders of giants".

ANGLAIS
Texte
In Defence of Laziness

All the evil in this world is brought about by persons who are always up and doing,[1] but do not know when they ought to be up nor what they ought to be doing. The devil, I take it, is still the busiest creature in the universe, and I can quite imagine him denouncing laziness and becoming angry at the smallest waste of time. The world, we all freely admit, is in a muddle,[2] but I for one do not think that it is laziness that has brought it to such a pass. It is not the active virtues that it lacks but the passive ones; it is capable of anything but kindness and a little steady thought. There is still plenty of energy in the world (there never were more fussy people about), but most of it is simply misdirected. If, for example, in July 1914, when there was some capital idling weather, everybody, emperors, kings, archdukes, statesmen, generals, journalists, had been suddenly smitten with an intense desire to do nothing, just to hang about in the sunshine and consume tobacco, then we should all have been much better off than we are now. But no, there must be no time wasted; something must be done. And, as we know, something was done. Again, suppose our statesmen, instead of rushing off to Versailles with a bundle of ill-digested notions and a great deal of energy to dissipate, had all taken a fortnight off, away from all correspondence and interviews and what not, and had simply lounged about on some hillside or other, apparently doing nothing for the first time in their energetic lives, then they might have gone to their so-called Peace Conference and come away again with their reputations still unsoiled and the affairs of the world in good trim.[3]

J. B. PRIESTLEY

[1] *up and doing*—full of activity.
[2] *a muddle*—a state of disorder and confusion.
[3] *in good trim*—in good condition.

Travail à faire par le candidat

I. COMMENTAIRE DIRIGÉ (sur 14 points)

1. In what sense can Priestley claim that "the devil is still the busiest creature in the universe"?
2. Why does Priestley speak of a "so-called Peace Conference"? From what you know of the consequences of the Versailles Treaty, do you think he is justified in using such terms?
3. Is Priestley talking quite seriously? Or is he being humorous? Support your opinion from examples taken from the text.
4. Imagine one or several cases when it might be better to be idle than overactive.

II. VERSION (sur 6 points)

Translate into French from "Again suppose our statesmen . . ." to ". . . the affairs of the world in good trim".

C. *FEDERAL REPUBLIC OF GERMANY*

In Germany there is a specialized modern-languages section. What follows relates to this section, but much of what is stated may refer also to other sections of the *Gymnasium* which do not have a bias to modern languages.

In general the *written examination* in English takes the form of *reproduction* of a text read orally and commentary—textual explanation, a précis of a passage with commentary, and free composition. In French the examination may be less demanding. It will be noted that there is no translation. *Free composition* is an exercise not very often set, and the candidates have no choice of the topic they have to treat, although this may be of a literary, historical, philosophical, political, or social nature, depending on previous class-work. The time allowance is generous—300 minutes (five hours), and a monolingual dictionary is permitted. The paper is assessed by the class teacher, whose appraisal is made according to the length of the composition, the number and gravity of the errors in spelling, vocabulary, and grammar, the adequacy of the style, including the use of idiomatic expressions, and the content. There is no special examination in *literature and civilization*.

Précis and commentary is not at present a very common examination exercise, but it is becoming more frequent. The passage to be summarized varies in length according to the type of prose: 500–600 words for the prose of argument or exposition, 600–800 words for narrative or descriptive prose. If no commentary is asked for, these passages may be about one-third longer. Whereas passages from plays or poetry are not set, such passages as extracts from essays or newspaper articles, political documents, or literary prose are usual. The exercise lasts 300 minutes (five hours). The examiner assesses according to whether the text has been sufficiently understood, whether the condensation of the text (usually to one third of the original length) has been adequate, and, where appropriate, according to the quality of the comment. The comments may take the form of an *explication de texte* or the form of a reaction of the candidate to the passage.

Explication de texte is also not a very common form of examination exercise. When it is set the piece for interpretation is usually about 400–500 words in length, and again 300 minutes (five hours) is allowed. The type of passage may be literary, historical, social, economic, political, or philosophical, but rarely scientific, and again the choice depends on previous class-work. The criticism required may be both internal and external to the passage set: for a literary text the stress is usually on internal criticism, whereas a social or political text usually requires substantial external criticism.

The most usual form of the written examination is *reproduction and commentary*. The passage chosen for reproduction is most commonly narrative prose, treating one or more problems of aspects of life. It should be noted that anecdotal prose is not permitted. The passage, which is between 1000 and 1200 words long, is read over twice to the candidates, and the taking of notes is not permitted. The time allowed is 300 minutes (five hours). The form that the comments asked from the candidates may take is that of interpreting the passage or expressing their own views on the subject.

There is no *dictation* exercise in the terminal examination.

The *oral examination* has as its main objective the testing of the candidate's command of the spoken word, his ability to comprehend and evaluate a text and to show an understanding for the foreign culture and civilization. It is considered that the written and oral examination supplement each other, because different skills are involved in each. Both have equal weighting in the final assessment. Adequate performance in the written examination is not a prerequisite for admission to the oral. The examiner, since he is always the candidate's teacher, knows him well, is familiar with his school record, and has already the results of the written examination. Only rarely, however, does he ask the candidate questions on what he has written in the written papers.

The examination should take on the form of a talk or dialogue. The candidate is assigned a text, which he may study for ten to twenty minutes beforehand, or a particular question. He is asked to read part of the passage aloud. The passage is usually 200–250 words in length and may be of prose, poetry, or drama. It is usually related to the topics dealt with in the previous two years. After the reading the candidate expounds upon it, and the examiner may then intervene to put additional questions to him upon aspects not touched upon, or to correct mistakes. A discussion may then ensue. Sometimes, in order to give the candidate a greater chance of acquitting himself well, two shorter passages are given him to prepare, or he may have to prepare one text and one general question. The discussion may often touch upon contemporary problems which arise out of the text, particularly if this is taken from a newspaper. Although the examiner is the candidate's class teacher, the whole examining committee (all the class teachers of the candidate in the final two years) are present. The chairman of the examining committee may also ask questions. A third teacher takes notes and acts as a control, but does not put questions to the candidate. The three members of the committee are responsible for the final oral assessment. The total length of the oral examination is roughly ten minutes per candidate.

No set marking scheme is laid down for the assessment of the oral. In general there is a combination of 'global' and detailed marking, and a rough division between content and language. For content, the understanding and knowledge of the text, the candidate's evaluation and comments upon it, are taken into consideration. For language, structure, grammar, vocabulary, use of idiom, pronunciation, and fluency are all considered. Whilst there is no specific weighting of these categories, comprehension, pronunciation, grammar, and use of vocabulary are regarded as fundamental, whereas accent, structure, use of idiom, fluency, and knowledge of subject-matter will contribute to a better grade. There is at present no assessment on the basis of tape-recordings. Standardization of assessment is obtained to some extent through the chairman of the examining committee— who may be the headmaster or a school-inspector—who attends oral examinations at various schools in the area.

While neither reading comprehension nor aural comprehension *per se* forms part of the terminal examination, although both are tested incidentally, the candidate may, if he so desire, write independently an essay during his final year (*Hausarbeit*). This dissertation may be between ten and forty pages in length and is on a subject related to modern languages. It may, for example, be a comparative study of various newspapers, a critical essay on a book or a series of books, or a comparison between a book and the film that may have been made based upon it. The assessment of this essay is taken into account in estimating his school work during the final year, and thus indirectly contributes to the result of the final examination. The work may also be discussed in the oral examination.

The marking of the written scripts is undertaken by the teacher who has taught the candidate in the last two years. Any script judged to be not up to standard has to be referred to a second examiner, also a teacher. If no concordant judgment is reached the script must be referred to the headmaster or chairman of the examination committee, who may, in fact, be the headmaster. No marking scheme for scripts is officially laid down, but teachers under training receive instruction in this respect, and the subject has been discussed in articles in influential journals—see *Der Fremdsprachliche Unterricht* 41, 1967, and *Praxis*, 21, 1968. External control of the marking only takes place when the procedure described above has failed to end in a decision: in such a case, the matter is referred to the regional educational authority,* where an examiner comes to a decision. In very rare cases an aggrieved candidate may appeal to an administrative court. If such a body finds that the procedural formalities of the examination were irregular (non-observance of regulations, lack of equality of chances, etc.), the examination must be held again.

Partial failure in the examination may be compensated. If a candidate fails in the written examination a good mark in the oral or for the class-work of the previous two years may compensate; for failure in the oral examination corresponding compensations apply.

Procedures in the Federal Republic seem to come very near the concept of the *examen-bilan* as formulated by Recteur Capelle and others: class-work, written and oral examinations are all taken into account. In the top two grades, for example, some eight written tests (*Klassenarbeiten*) are given, which in kind and extent are similar to the questions set in the final examination and are assessed by the class teacher for English. In addition, oral attainment is systematically assessed in the last two years on the basis of classroom performance. Pupils receive three reports (*Zeugnisse*) during this period at half-yearly intervals, and since these are made available to the examiners for the final examination, their progress can be easily evaluated. In this connection it is therefore possible to speak of continuous assessment.

In an attempt to arrive at some criteria for the evaluation of both oral and written proficiency in modern languages a group of experts convened by the Council of Europe in 1969 agreed upon the following document, which postulates six criteria each divided into seven levels. For convenience a French translation is also appended.(3)

---

* In Hesse there are two such authorities: *Regierungspräsident Darmstadt* and *Regierungspräsident Kassel*.

Suggested Criteria for the Evaluation of Oral and Written Proficiency in Modern Languages

Six criteria are postulated:

A. Pronunciation and Accent (for oral proficiency only)
B. Grammar and Structure
C. Vocabulary and Idiom
D. Fluency
E. Comprehension
F. Subject-matter

Each of these criteria is evaluated on a seven-point ascending scale. Since the scale is hierarchical, it is assumed that proficiency at any given level upon it includes proficiency at all levels inferior to that level.

Criteria

A. *Pronunciation and Accent*

  1. Very 'foreign', almost unintelligible
  2. Very laboured. Numerous errors and hesitations
  3. Inconsistent and faltering—*e.g.*, phonemes, intonation, stress
  4. Satisfactory speed and intonation, in spite of some inaccuracies
  5. Few errors and hesitations
  6. Ease and accuracy
  7. Hardly distinguishable from normal speech of native speaker

B. *Grammar and Structure*

  1. Very many grammatical errors. Almost total ignorance of structures
  2. Still deficiencies in elementary structures
  3. Elementary structures known. Use sometimes inaccurate
  4. More complex structures. More accurate use
  5. Wider range. Few inaccuracies
  6. Almost complete command of structures
  7. Knowledge comparable to that of cultured native speaker

C. *Vocabulary and Idiom*

  1. Completely rudimentary
  2. Very elementary
  3. Elementary and trivial. Not sufficiently diverse
  4. Satisfactory and appropriate
  5. Varied and usually accurate in use
  6. Rich and varied
  7. Comparable to that of cultured native speaker

D. *Fluency*

  1. Negligible
  2. Disjointed and hesitant

3. Uneven
4. Satisfactory though somewhat erratic
5. Rarely hesitant
6. Great facility
7. Comparable to that of cultured native speaker

E. *Comprehension*

1. Nil to fragmentary
2. Laboured and incomplete
3. Slow and necessitating simple language
4. Generally correct response
5. Good overall understanding
6. Good understanding of the whole and of shades of meaning
7. Perfect understanding

F. *Subject Matter*

1. Almost complete lack of knowledge
2. Insufficient knowledge
3. Knowledge still vague, sometimes inaccurate and irrelevant
4. Knowledge limited. Subject-matter relevant
5. Good range of knowledge and ideas
6. Wide knowledge. Material well organized
7. Outstandingly good, displaying judgment and critical sense

CRITÈRES D'ÉVALUATION

A. *Prononciation et accent*

1. Très 'étrangère', presque inintelligible
2. Très laborieuse. Erreurs et hésitations nombreuses
3. Inégale et incertaine (*ex.* phonèmes, intonation, accent tonique)
4. Débit et intonation suffisants malgré certaines inexactitudes
5. Erreurs et hésitations peu nombreuses
6. Facilité et exactitude
7. Ne se distingue guère du parler courant d'un autochtone

B. *Grammaire et structures*

1. Erreurs grammaticales très nombreuses. Ignorance quasi totale des structures
2. Structures élémentaires encore défectueuses
3. Structures élémentaires connues. Emploi parfois incertain
4. Structures plus complexes. Emploi plus sûr
5. Éventail plus étendu. Erreurs peu nombreuses
6. Maîtrise presque complète des structures
7. Connaissance comparable à celle d'un autochtone cultivé

C. *Lexique*

1. Tout à fait rudimentaire

   2. Très élémentaire
   3. Élémentaire. Peu varié
   4. Suffisant et relativement juste
   5. Varié et d'un emploi généralement juste
   6. Riche et nuancé
   7. Comparable à celui d'un autochtone cultivé

D. *Expression spontanée*

   1. Inexistante ou presque
   2. Décousue, hésitante
   3. Inégale
   4. Suffisante malgré une certaine irrégularité
   5. Rarement hésitante ou fautive
   6. Grande aisance
   7. Comparable à celle d'un autochtone cultivé

E. *Compréhension*

   1. Nulle ou trop fragmentaire
   2. Laborieuse et incomplète
   3. Lente et requérant une langue simplifiée
   4. Réaction généralement correcte
   5. Bonne compréhension de l'ensemble
   6. Bonne compréhension de l'ensemble et des nuances
   7. Compréhension parfaite

F. *Étude de contenu*

   1. Absence quasi totale de connaissances et d'idées
   2. Connaissances et idées insuffisantes
   3. Connaissances encore vagues, parfois inexactes ou sans rapport avec le sujet. Quelques idées
   4. Connaissances limitées. Des idées. Le sujet est traité
   5. Bon éventail de connaissances et d'idées
   6. Connaissances étendues, idées justes, bonne présentation
   7. Étude excellente relevant jugement et sens critique

It is evident that in the evaluation of written skills in modern languages Western Europe is entering upon a period of experiment and innovation. A good examination should be a stimulus to the pupil. Few would claim that the traditional type of examination was in fact this, save for the very best pupils. What is required is a greater systematization, an up-dating of old practices and, above all, the setting of exercises that will test the candidate's creative and imaginative ability and at the same time demonstrate his command of the language as an instrument for everyday use. Much of what has been said holds good also for the evaluation of oral competence, to which we must now turn.

CHAPTER 6—NOTES

(1) A. Davies, "Language Proficiency Testing", paper given at *Sixth International Conference on Second Language Problems* in Dublin in March 1965.

(2) Marklund, Henrysson, and Paulin, *Studieprognos och studieframgång* (Stockholm: Statens Offentliga Utredningar, 1968), p. 203 *et seq.*

(3) At a Council of Europe conference on "Continuous Assessment", held at Sundsvall, Sweden, in July 1969.

Oral Evaluation

The accent being placed upon oral skills in languages has meant that there is increasing interest in how they should be evaluated— although at present Cyprus, Finland, Ireland, and Spain do not test this in their final academic secondary leaving examination. In other countries oral testing generally conforms to a very similar pattern. The practice is usually for the candidate to be given a short time beforehand in which to study a text, usually of a literary nature. He is then called upon to read it aloud to the examiner and to reply spontaneously to questions posed upon it. This particular questioning may lead on to a short 'conversation' (in practice, often the extension merely of the questioning approach) of a more general nature which may relate to the literature, culture, and general knowledge of the country whose language is being studied. Candidates are usually examined individually, and the average length of the testing is between ten and twenty minutes. There is little detailed structuring of the examination, and examiners tend to rely on a 'global' impression in order to arrive at the final mark. (Table 13 gives comparative details of how the examination is carried out in a number of countries.) This traditional pattern of oral examining has held good for at least a generation. Some experiments are being carried on, however, as to the tape-recording of candidates—in Belgium and England, for example—so that evaluation may take place later, either with several examiners, or as a check on the mark arrived at in the face-to-face situation. The impression is, however, that both examiners and teachers tend to be sceptical of their own ability in assessing oral competence with any degree of accuracy. This is reflected in the comparatively little weight still given to the oral examination in arriving at a candidate's final mark for the complete examination in languages. A general move, however, is being made to strengthen the oral test so as to increase its reliability and validity, and thus allow it to count for more. The difficulties encountered in doing so are nevertheless great and must be looked at in detail.

One must first define what are the objectives of an oral examination in languages. What are, in fact, the particular oral skills or knowledge that require to be tested by oral means? On the whole, if such an assessment can be arrived at by using written means, then it is plainly preferable to do so. This would, for example, preclude the testing of knowledge of literature in an oral examination. It has been argued that this is the only means one has of ensuring that the candidate has in fact covered the whole literature syllabus, and not just those authors or works on which he has chosen to answer questions in the written papers. This argument lacks validity. A short-answer or multiple-choice test, which tested pure knowledge only of the literature syllabus, extending over its whole range, would surely be preferable. The overriding purposes of an oral examination are surely rather to test the application of knowledge, to synthesize its various facets, and to manipulate elegantly and meaningfully the foreign language. Of the importance of oral expression—or *oracy*—there can be do doubt; nor can there be of the importance of testing comprehension in spontaneous conversation, although such comprehension should also be more formally tested in a listening comprehension test. Certainly the capacity for oral expression, to 'think on one's feet' whilst addressing an audience, or engaged in a dialogue or a conversation, is one that is rightly highly valued in the modern world—and even more so when the speaker is talking in a foreign language. The danger to be guarded against is one to be watched also in a conventional intelligence test: this form of examination may unduly favour the superficial, articulate, and fluent improviser as against the more profound, reflective, and sustained thinker who performs better when he commits his ideas to paper. If, in some respects, the oral examination is a test of personality and maturity the examiner must use great perception and skill in order to evaluate the candidate fairly. He must exercise a fine judgment in order to discover how efficiently the candidate can *apply* what he has learnt, which constitutes the positively creative aspect of language learning.

Unfortunately there are many pitfalls open to the inexperienced examiner. He may himself exhibit unconscious bias. Oral examining as a unique case of social or dyadic interaction is subject more than most situations to what has been termed 'the personal equation'. There is a 'halo' tendency, perhaps exemplified when a striking trait that the examiner particularly esteems is exhibited by the candidate, whether or not this trait is relevant to the assessment. In such a case the examiner may be unduly generous in the mark that he finally awards. Conversely, if the trait is disliked by the examiner he may

Table 13—The oral examination (general)

	Bg	Cy	Dk	Ge	Fi	Fr	Ir	It	Ma	Lux(5)	Neth	Sp	Tu	UK(E)
Does examiner have pre-knowledge of candidate?	Yes(1)	No oral exam.	No	Yes(1)	No oral exam.	Sometimes	No oral exam. except for Irish	Yes	No	Yes	Yes	No	Yes(1)	No
Is the oral exam. structured?	Yes		Yes	Yes		Yes		No	Yes	No(6)	Yes	No	Yes	No
No. of candidates examined simultaneously	One		One	One		One		One	One	One	One	One	One	One
No. of examiners present	One		Two	At least three		One		Two or three	One	One	Two	Two or more	Three	One
Use of tape-recorder	Yes(2)		No	No		No		No	No	Sometimes	No	No	No	No
Pre-selection of questions	Yes		Yes (4)	Yes		No		No	No	No	No	No	No	Possibly
Time allowed for exam.	15 mins.			10–12 mins.		No 15 mins.		15–20 mins.	10 mins.	15± mins.	20 mins.	3–4 mins. [sic]	20 mins.	10 mins.
Time allowed for preparation	Yes		15 mins.	Yes (10–20 mins.)		Yes (15 mins.)		?	None	5–10 mins. (if given)	15 mins.	No	10 mins.	5 mins.
Does candidate read a passage aloud?	Yes(2)		Yes	Yes		Yes		Yes	Yes	Mostly	Yes	Yes	Yes	Yes
Use of pictures	No(3)		No	No		No		No	No	No	No	No	Yes	No
Discussion	No(3)		Yes	Yes		Yes		Yes(2)	Yes(2)	Yes	Yes	Yes	No	Possibly
General conversation	No(3)		No	No(2)		No(2)		Yes	Yes	No	Yes	Yes	Yes(2)	Yes
Is there a special Aural Comprehension test?	No(3)		No	No		No		No	No(2)	No	No	No	No	No

be unduly severe. Too often examiners seek to judge what might be termed general qualities—perhaps those they esteem necessary for success in higher education—rather than concentrate on linguistic capacity. It has been shown that interviewers who work in a similar situation to that of the oral examiner are often unduly influenced by irrelevant factors such as social origins, religion, dress, or physical appearance. The suggestion has been made that to counteract prejudice the oral examiner should be provided with as much background information as possible regarding the candidate. But such knowledge might merely confirm the examiner's bias instead of nullifying it. In any case, such background information itself, if it takes the form of comments from teachers, may itself be partly the result of prejudice, unless it is confined to purely factual statements such as that "during the past year the candidate has undergone three tests of a non-objective nature, as a result of which he was placed sixth in a rank order of a class of thirty-six".

The second tendency apparent in many examiners is what has been described as the 'generosity' or 'leniency' tendency. This may become especially apparent in an oral 'confrontation' in which emotional reactions must inevitably develop between the candidate and the examiner. Reuchlin, for oral examinations in general, has shown that in a face-to-face situation the examiner tends to award more marks to the candidate than when he is asked to evaluate the performance of the same candidate recorded on videotape. It is also true that when an examiner is asked to mark a candidate purely on the evidence of a tape-recording of an oral examination—*i.e.*, without seeing the candidate—he will prove even less generous. If—and this for obvious reasons can apply only marginally to oral examinations in languages—he is merely supplied with a transcript of what the candidate said at an oral examination—he will tend to mark the least generously.

Another form that subjectivity in evaluation may take is what has been described as 'central tendency'. This consists in avoiding very good or very bad marks. By playing safe and not using the whole

---

Notes to Table 13 opposite

(1) The teacher tests his own pupils.
(2) Occasionally.
(3) These will be introduced when reforms are completed.
(4) 30 minutes for English and German, 20 minutes for French.
(5) Oral only in second attempt if failed in only one main subject.
(6) On the authors and texts studied in class.
    The teacher carries it out as he likes.

range of the marking scale it will be seen that all assessments approximate too closely to the median. This tendency may be due either to the inadequacy of the testing techniques employed or because the examiner is unsure of himself and exercises over-caution in his judgment.

How may these forms of subjectivity, which usually work in favour of the weaker candidate (and therefore penalize the better candidate by rating him too near his fellows) be eliminated? There is much argument in Europe as to whether *in the examining situation* the oral examiner should have any knowledge of the candidate's background. The Germans, for example, claim that he should. (The qualification regarding the examining situation is important. It is becoming increasingly recognized that, in the final overall assessment of a candidate, and in particular to help in predicting his future capabilities in higher education, all available evidence in the form of a 'balance-sheet' of positive assets and negative liabilities must be taken into account—hence the French concept of the *examen-bilan*.) Bias may be neutralized perhaps by having two or more examiners undertake the oral examination together—but if only two are employed one may 'dominate' the judgment of the other. Another alternative may be to give a group examination to the candidates. It is argued that the fact of having other candidates present as a yardstick against which to evaluate linguistic performance may mitigate, if not eliminate, personal bias against any one of them. The danger is again that one may be evaluating personality traits as well. The timid pupil would not shine because he would not get sufficient chance to talk. If time and facilities were available, if fluency were considered an important goal, the oral examination could be supplemented by recording in a language laboratory an *exposé* lasting some ten minutes on a topic that they had been given a similar length of time to prepare for immediately before the oral examination. These tapes would then be evaluated centrally by a group of examiners.

As it is, all the research evidence shows that oral examiners are unreliable. A study by Trimble(1) proved that they even failed to agree substantially on the rank order in which they should place the candidates, leaving aside the question of how much each candidate was worth on some absolute scale, a decision that is vital in determining whether he should go on to higher education. Other studies by Valin(2), and Piéron, Reuchlin, and Bacher(3) also highlight this unreliability. These demonstrated, for example, that there was very small correlation in the results of oral and written examinations. On the other hand, it could be argued that for modern languages this would be no bad thing, because both forms of the examination should be testing different skills. But, contrary to what has arisen in some small experiments in which the present writer has helped, there should certainly not be a *negative* correlation. On the whole candidates who are good at written expression should also be good at oral expression.

That national authorities agree on the desirability of emphasizing more effectively oral work by giving it increased importance in examinations is evident. In England *Schools Council Working Paper No. 2* postulated:

> If it is an important aim of good teaching to train pupils to sustain a point of view in speech and to be an active participant in the dialectic of teaching and learning, then it would seem anomalous that the examination should ignore this entirely.

The oral examination is looked upon as having a beneficial effect upon teaching method, encouraging audio-lingual and audio-visual techniques not only at the lower levels, but also at the upper levels of language learning. Oral assessment cannot therefore be omitted. Consequently what practical steps can be taken to improve its reliability and validity?

As previously mentioned, one must begin by defining with some precision the particular skills or knowledge one is attempting to evaluate. In the main these may be summed up as relating to pronunciation and accent, grammar and structure (including style), vocabulary and idiom (including intelligibility, style, and relevance), fluency and speed (including relevance again), comprehension and subject matter. (It is too often forgotten that every oral examination is by definition a test of *speed*: candidates must answer questions in the order in which they are presented by the examiner, and not, as in a written examination of the conventional kind, with time for reflection and latitude to answer questions in any order he pleases. Furthermore, even content needs to be more clearly spelt out. Construct validity will depend, as in the written examination, on what is the type of 'terminal behaviour' aimed at. This should perhaps be done by setting out a number of 'linguistic situations' in which the candidate should feel at home. Once the skills and knowledge to be evaluated have been elaborated, a next step is to produce a rating scale for scoring them. Such a rating scale was given in the last chapter—*see* page 80. Worked out by a group of language experts from a number of countries attending a Council of Europe conference at Sundsvall, Sweden, it may claim to have some international consensus behind it. But it remains one of a number of such scales that could be devised. Another such rating scale is that of the Foreign Service Institute, Washington, D.C.—*see* Table 14. In any

Table 14—Levels of oral proficiency (Foreign Service Institute, Washington D.C.)

	S-1 Elementary Proficiency	S-2 Limited Work Proficiency	S-3 Minimal Professional Proficiency	S-4 Full Professional Proficiency	S-5 Native or Bilingual
Pronunciation	Often unintelligible	Usually foreign but rarely unintelligible	Sometimes foreign but always intelligible		Native
Grammar	Accuracy limited to set expressions, almost no control of syntax; often wrong information	Fair control of most basic syntactic patterns; conveys meaning accurately in simple sentences most of time	Good control of most basic syntactic patterns; always conveys meaning accurately in reasonably complex sentences	Makes only occasional errors, and these show no pattern of deficiency	Native
Vocabulary	Adequate only for survival, travel, and basic needs	Adequate for simple social conversation and routine job needs	Adequate for participation in all general conversation and for professional discussions in a special field	Professional and general vocabulary broad and precise, appropriate to occasion	Equal to vocabulary of an educated native speaker
Fluency	Except for memorized expressions, every utterance requires enormous, obvious effort	Usually hesitant; often forced to silence by limitation of grammar and vocabulary	Rarely hesitant; always able to sustain conversation through circumlocutions	Speech on all professional matters as apparently effortless as in mother tongue, always easy to listen to	Speech at least as fluent and effortless as mother tongue, on all occasions
Comprehension	May require much repetition, slow rate of speech; understands only very short utterances	Understands in general non-technical speech directed to him, but sometimes misinterpreted or needs utterances reworded. Usually cannot follow conversation between native speakers	Understands most of what is said to him; can follow speeches, clear radio broadcasts, most conversations between native speakers	Can understand all educated speech in any context; occasionally baffled by colloquialisms and regionalisms	Equal to that of the native speaker

case, such scales would require internal 'weighting': a coefficient of importance must be given to each division of skills or knowledge that requires to be tested. This 'weighting' may—and should—vary according to the aims of the examination. Only in this way can a valid evaluation instrument be devised.

A next step consists in devising suitable material to test each of the skills or knowledge. In general, it is preferable that skills should be tested separately. Thus the candidate has the chance to show his capabilities in a whole variety of tests: phonetic discrimination test, listening comprehension test, general conversation and discussion, general pronunciation test (*e.g.*, the reading of a prepared and an unprepared passage), the *exposé* (either uninterrupted or with interventions and interpolations by the examiner to which the candidate must react), renarration, and reading comprehension. Depending on the time available, oral fluency can be tested in a more elaborate way. Each candidate could study a flash-card showing a simple picture for about half a minute. He would then be required to speak on the picture for a further half minute in any way he pleased. He might merely give a description, recount the story he imagines it relates, comment on it, or continue the story as he wishes. This would be recorded. His speech could then he evaluated from a number of viewpoints: pronunciation, morphology, vocabulary, and, in particular, the number of intelligible clauses spoken. Inappropriate hesitations would be penalized. Each of these factors would be weighted, but the emphasis in evaluation would be on the number and quality of intelligible clauses spoken by the candidate.

Some indication of how this might work out in detail can be gained from considering the new procedures for oral examining in Sweden, which consist of a battery of tests. The first two of these are reading tests. One consists of a piece of conversation containing some thirty lines of brief dialogue, for the reading of which the candidate is given only forty-five seconds of preparation time. The reading is recorded, and scored later in a standardized way, with only certain phonemes in each line of dialogue being taken into account. The second reading test consists of some fifteen lines of prose, also mainly of conversation, but with longer sentences. For this the pupil has one minute to prepare. Unlike the first reading test, it is scored on 'global' impression, the idea being to obtain:

> . . . an overall picture of the pupil's ability to reproduce language that sounds genuinely English. Thus general quality of intonation, pronunciation, rhythm, and fluency is to be judged as a whole while occasional errors of pronunciation should be disregarded.(4)

The other two oral tests are a speaking test and an oral production test. The object of the speaking test is to measure the pupil's ability to speak without interruption for about a minute on a subject that he knows well. This might include, for example, the description of a friend or acquaintance. The pupil is allowed thirty seconds' preparation, and then records his effort. The second test of oral production is based on a picture from which the pupil has to make up a story. It might show, for example, what happens when a Scotsman attempts to smuggle goods (duty-free whisky?) back into Britain after a holiday abroad, and is held up by a customs officer. For this test also thirty seconds' preparation is allowed, and the pupil is given one and a half minutes in which to record his effort. Both these tests are scored on 'global' impressions of the pupil's ability:

> . . . to convey pertinent information efficiently and adequately . . . oral production is therefore to be judged from two aspects: (*a*) *contents*—amount and relevance of information conveyed; (*b*) *command of language*—adequate use of words and structures, fluency, richness, and variety of expression.(4)

It goes without saying that pupils have some instruction in how to tackle these tests before the examination proper arrives. The examples given are taken from actual tests administered to eighth grade pupils in the general course—*i.e.*, to pupils aged about fifteen in the Swedish unitary school.

Other modes of examining are, of course, also possible. It might be desirable to examine candidates in pairs, launching them after a suitable 'warming-up' period into a discussion in which the examiner would intervene only when he considered the dialogue was flagging and needed stimulating. The sequence of question and mumbled answer—too often monosyllabic—between examiner and candidate, which is at present the rule, can hardly be said to constitute a dialogue (for which in any case time is too often lacking), and can hardly be said to probe the depths of the candidate's skill and understanding in the foreign language. Whilst a stressful situation should normally be avoided, there is surely great merit in the examiner systematically evaluating, by increasing the degree of difficulty of his questions progressively, what is the limit of a candidate's linguistic competence. There should also be some opportunity for the examiner to intervene with the unexpected, in order to find out how the candidate reacts spontaneously to a novel idea or situation in the foreign language. All this places a great burden upon the single examiner, who has both to examine and assess at the same time. In certain circumstances it might be advisable for a second person to be present to act as assessor. It is also desirable that in discussion a candidate should be allowed free rein to lead the conversation in the direction of topics on which he would like to speak, and that later this procedure should be reversed.

It must be admitted that complete objectivity in oral examining is virtually unobtainable. American procedures, which employ exclusively 'pencil and paper' tests of the objective kind, measure only passive oral skills. They are not completely acceptable to language examiners in Europe familiar with them, because a vital element of spontaneity and individualization is, it is alleged, removed from the evaluation. If, as has been proposed, the proportion of marks awarded in an oral examination may rise as high as 40 per cent a drastic reshaping of its main features, together with the possibility of using *some* objective tests, must nevertheless take place. There is no doubt that some aspects of oral proficiency, such as the ability to generate meaningful grammatical structures creatively, will always elude exact measurement. But the stricter observance of a taxonomy of objectives, the adherence to a uniform structure and to an exact scoring scheme, should yield a more equitable result. Such a truly Cartesian division of the task does not of itself render the examination more objective, but it has at least the great merit of impressing upon those responsible for the evaluation process all the different facets of the candidate's performance that have to be evaluated, and the mistakes that may arise in so doing.

CHAPTER 7—NOTES

(1) O. C. Trimble, "The Oral Examination: its Validity and Reliability," *School and Society* (New York, 1934, No. 1009, Vol. 39, pp. 550–552).
(2) E. Valin, *La valeur des examens*, étude docimologique réalisée au Liban. UNESCO—études et documents d'éducation.
(3) H. Piéron, M. Reuchlin, and F. Bacher, "Une recherche expérimentale de docimologie sur les examens oraux de physique au niveau du baccalauréat de mathématiques", *Biotypologie*, March–June 1962.
(4) *Test Instructions*, National Board of Education, Stockholm.

Chapter 8
Some Conclusions

From this brief survey of language teaching in Western Europe there can be discerned an increasing systematization in teaching methodology reinforced by the contributions of applied linguistics and ancillary aids. The first great linguistic revolution at the turn of the century, accomplished by men such as Jespersen and Sweet, had little lasting effect on classroom practice. A minority of enthusiastic teachers struggled gallantly on with the so-called 'Direct Method', or its modification, the 'Oral Method'. Not until after the Second World War did a new wave of enthusiasm for language teaching and learning sweep Western Europe. For those countries who bore the main shock of war, either being occupied by the Germans or receiving Allied troops later, learning a smattering of a foreign language was often a positive advantage in the struggle for existence. With the return of peacetime conditions interest grew again: new research into the learning of languages, this time backed by the new technology, flourished. Results became manifest in the 1960s when the universalization of secondary education implied that all should be taught a foreign language. Meanwhile Piagetian theories of early learning had induced many to experiment in the primary school.

Despite such advances it must still be admitted that a knowledge of how languages are acquired remains fragmentary. We may be helped when we have discovered more about the way in which a young child learns his mother tongue. At present we still flounder as to the correct pedagogical order in which linguistic concepts should be taught. We now recognize that frequency is only one among a number of possible criteria. The massive support that can be given by applied linguistics is still to come. Similarly, in the field of psycholinguistics we cannot yet identify completely the important factors. Is Skinnerian psychology the answer to our problems, or do children become so bored by its applications that they fail to learn?

The attainment of bilingualism in Western Europe by 1980 will depend largely on the quantity and quality of teachers available. Although the problem of numbers now seems nearer solution, we have perhaps as yet paid insufficient attention to the quality of teacher training, the first condition of which is the acquisition of linguistic competence. Further practical steps to help this could be taken almost immediately. Tables 15 and 16 show the number of foreign assistants in Britain and other countries during the academic year 1968–69 and previous years. Despite the strenuous efforts, limited nearly always by financial considerations, to increase numbers made by the official and semi-official bodies entrusted with the organization of exchanges, the number of foreign assistants in schools remains woefully low. The United Kingdom sent only 1390 assistants abroad. The number of English-speaking assistants from the other English-speaking countries—the U.S.A. and the Commonwealth—is comparatively negligible. France, as the main source of supply for French-speaking assistants, sent out 2715—considerably more—but the bulk of these came to the United Kingdom. German assistants sent abroad numbered 957, and were divided almost evenly between the United Kingdom and France. Admittedly, these numbers do not include the potential language teachers who spend some time of their university course studying in the foreign country, but the figures are indicative.(1)

The nature of the university course is a stumbling-block in the preparation of secondary teachers. Most students of *Anglistik* at German universities do become teachers of English. In France the proportion of students of English becoming teachers is less, but higher than in England, where only about half the graduates in modern languages return to the schools to teach their subject. In all three countries the course is not really designed to produce modern-language teachers—there is in fact no reason why it should do so, because modern languages is a university discipline in its own right. But the undue concentration on literature and on philology—in its old-fashioned meaning—has the result of producing future language teachers who are not particularly linguistically competent, especially in the spoken language. A first step to rectify this would be to insist that before entering upon a teacher-training course all students should be required to spend at least a year abroad. As part of their education as teachers they would follow courses in phonetics and general and applied linguistics, as well as in contemporary culture and civilization. These courses would supplement those on methodology and teaching practice.

That much of this kind of training might even be done without residence abroad is evidenced by the case of the U.S.S.R., which in 1968–69 sent only eighty-three assistants abroad. Although their

Table 15—Great Britain: Language assistants 1968/69 as at 20th January 1969

ENGLAND WALES, NORTHERN IRELAND

Foreign Assistants

Algerian	12
Austrian	27
Belgian	16
French	2036
German	480
Italian	14
Moroccan	12
Spanish	199
Swiss	31
Tunisian	18
	—— 2845

British Assistants

Austria	33
Belgium	3
France	854
Germany	239
Italy	14
Spain	49
Switzerland	14
Tunisia	0
	—— 1206

	TOTAL	4051

Total applications processed:

Foreign	3943
British	1450
	—— 5393

SCOTLAND

Foreign Assistants

France	205
Germany	49
Switzerland	—
Austria	1
Italy	—
Spain	21
	—— 276

Scottish Assistants

France	138	
Germany	31	
Switzerland	1	
Austria	4	
Italy	5	
Spain	5	
	—	184
TOTAL		460

approach to language-teaching may be considered to be over-utilitarian, the Soviet teacher-training institutions give courses which are geared from the beginning to preparing teachers. The largest of these institutions is the State Institute for Foreign Languages in Moscow, whose full time course usually lasts five years. Separate departments exist for English, French, and German. (There is also an Interpreters' Department, which covers a wide range of languages.) During their training intending teachers of English (which is the foreign language most widely taught in Russian schools) receive 2000 hours of instruction in the language. In the first year as much as twenty-two hours a week is devoted to this alone. There is also a programme in linguistics, which includes phonetics, stylistics, grammar, the history of the language, and general linguistics; a course in Latin (since no Latin is taught in Soviet secondary schools); and a course in the literature, history, and geography of the English-speaking peoples. These are supplemented by courses in a second foreign language (of which German is the most usual), in psychology and pedagogics, and in Soviet economics, philosophy, and history. One weakness is that only ten weeks of the course is devoted to teaching practice. There is comparatively little stress upon literature, the teaching of which does not begin until the fourth year. On the other hand, students are expected to be able to converse fluently upon a variety of topics, including technological and industrial affairs. For posts in some schools where English is a special feature they are also required to be able to teach other curricular subjects, such as history and geography, in English.

Nevertheless, whatever the shortcomings of the present system of training (and in England the Schools Council has just commissioned an inquiry into the training of language teachers), European secondary teachers will have had much greater 'exposure' to the foreign language than their primary colleagues. Yet, if efforts towards bilingualism are to succeed, this can only mean that the foreign language must begin in the primary school. Drastic measures are required to upgrade the quality of the teachers enlisted with this vital task.

Table 16—Foreign Language Assistant Statistics: countries and languages involved
(figures given by receiving countries)

Receiving Country	Year	A UK	B Fr	C Ger	D Sp	E It	F Aus	G Sw	H Bel	I Alg	J Mor	K Tun	L USA	M C'th	N Rus Sp Cts	O Others	Total
France	66-67	927[f]		—	—	—	—	—	0	0	0	0	54	87	—	0	1068
	67-68	948[f]		428[g]	256	84	—	—	0	0	0	0	55	84	80	1[h], 3[i]	1939
	68-69	984[f]		410	265	79	30	9	0	0	0	0	70	99	81	3[i], 9[j]	2039
Germany	66-67	254	191		5	5	0	1[k]	2	0	0	0	42	9	0	0	509
	67-68	230	247		7	4	0	1[k]	0	0	0	0	49	10	0	0	548
	68-69	264	283		7	4	0	1[k]	0	0	0	0	34	8	0	0	601
Spain	66-67	43	6	0		0	0	0	0	0	0	0	0	0	0	0	49
	67-68	54	14	0		0	0	0	0	0	0	0	0	0	0	0	68
	68-69	42	46	2			0	0	0	0	0	0	0	0	0	0	90
Italy	66-67	9	68	5	5		4	0	0	0	0	0	0	0	0	0	91
	67-68	15	67	5	4		4	0	0	0	0	0	0	0	0	0	95
	68-69	18	74	7	5		3	0	0	0	0	0	0	0	0	0	107
Austria	66-67	36	25	0	0	5		0	0	0	0	0	0	0	0	0	66
	67-68	37	26	0	0	6		0	0	0	0	0	0	0	0	0	69
	68-69	36	30	0	0	2		0	0	0	0	0	0	0	0	0	68
Switzerland	66-67	8	0	0	0	0	0		0	0	0	0	0	0	0	0	8
	67-68	10	0	0	0	0	0		0	0	0	0	0	0	0	0	10
	68-69	13	0	0	0	0	0		0	0	0	0	0	0	0	0	13
Belgium	66-67	3	0	3	0	0	0	0		0	0	0	0	0	0	0	6
	67-68	3	0	3	0	0	0	0		0	0	0	0	0	0	0	6
	68-69	3	0	3	0	0	0	0		0	0	0	0	0	0	0	6

		A	B	C	D	E	F	G	H	I	J	K	L	M	N	O	Total
England and Wales	66–67	1546	368	139	10	17	21	2	0	6	0	0	0	0	0	0	2109
	67–68	1807	429	169	12	29	39	8	2	6	0	0	0	0	1[a]	1[b]	2503
	68–69	2034	480[c]	194[d]	14	27	31	16	12	10	18	0	2[e]	0	2[a]	1[b]	2846
Scotland	66–67	173	51	11	1	2	0	0	0	0	0	0	0	0	0	0	238
	67–68	185	58	13	3	5	1	0	0	0	0	0	0	0	0	0	265
	68–69	205	49	21	0	1	0	0	0	0	0	0	0	0	0	0	276
N. Ireland	66–67	32	7	4	0	0	0	0	0	0	0	0	0	0	0	0	43
	67–68	41	9	4	0	0	0	0	1	1	0	0	0	0	0	1[l]	57
	68–69	41	6	7	0	0	0	0	0	2	0	0	0	0	0	0	56
UK Total	66–67	1578	375	143	10	17	21	2	0	6	0	0	0	0	0	0	2152
	67–68	2033	496	186	15	34	40	8	3	7	0	0	0	0	1	2	2825
	68–69	2282	535	227	14	28	31	16	12	12	18	0	0	0	2	1[l]	3178

A. U.K.
B. France.
C. Germany.
D. Spain.
E. Italy.
F. Austria.
G. Switzerland.
H. Belgium.
I. Algeria.
J. Morocco.
K. Tunisia.
L. U.S.A.
M. Commonwealth.
N. Russian-speaking Countries.
O. Others.

Notes

— No statistics supplied.
a. Russian-speaking.
b. Hebrew-speaking.
c. Includes one from Liechtenstein.
d. Includes one each from Argentina, Colombia, and Uruguay.
e. Canada.
f. U.K. Assistants only.
g. All German-speaking countries.
h. South Africa.
i. 1 Chinese, 1 Arabian, 1 Czech.
j. English-language Assistants.
k. Suisse-Romande.
l. French-speaking (Congo).

There are some who question in any case the wisdom of this early beginning unless special measures are taken to diminish the risks. In France there is a call to reinforce the teaching of the mother tongue if teaching of the foreign language is to be generalized in the primary school. The true bilingual, as distinct from the ambilingual, is in any case very rare. What one must aim to do is to see that the young child is given a solid foundation first in his mother tongue. The viewpoint of many in France is expressed by Pierre Burney: "We are in favour of the early teaching of foreign languages, but against teaching them prematurely."(2)

What will be the effect of bilingualism in Europe on the English language itself? The strain put upon it will undoubtedly be great. The British Council Annual Report for 1969 stated that "unremitting efforts will be needed to keep local variants of second language English within the bounds of comprehensibility". It was referring in this context more to the developing countries. Already the Indian who takes up a teaching post in Northern Nigeria may find that the English spoken by his Nigerian students is incomprehensible to him. Within India itself the dialects of English spoken in West Bengal and Kerala are not mutually understandable. Likewise, the Caribbean Creole dialect of English and the Polynesian Pidgin spoken in the Far East have almost become languages in their own right. It is not, however, expected that the situation within Europe could develop in this way. It may be more akin to that of the United States at the turn of the century after successive waves of immigration. The ability of English to survive in the face of other competing languages is one of the miracles of language. As Denis Brogan has written of America:

> The creation of general literacy and a common written and spoken tongue, intelligible everywhere except possibly in the deep South, is an achievement as remarkable as the creation of Mandarin Chinese or Low Latin or Hellenistic Greek, and this tongue is certain to be the new *lingua franca* of the world.(3)

The English spoken in America managed, as the English spoken in Britain in the past, to assimilate and turn to good use the extraneous influences of other tongues. Likewise the impact of Europeans all speaking English can also be absorbed and prove a source of enrichment to the language. But the danger of incomprehensibility must still be reckoned with.

Finally, we do not know what would be the ultimate outcome of a bilingual European society, for language is the most potent cultural factor of all. The Englishman visiting the United States for the first time feels more at home in a few hours than he does after a lifetime of visits to France, however well he may know the French language. This is because language conditions our attitudes, sets bounds upon our thinking, generates our values, and decides the quality of our life. The new bilingual European will have added a new dimension to his existence, the consequences of which are unforeseeable. It is perhaps regrettable that, despite the laudable efforts of the French to promote their own language, it is English that will prevail. As the British Council Report previously referred to remarks: "It is not only the main language of debate at the United Nations, but also the language of computers, of nuclear science, of Japanese salesmen, and many others." That this is due to American and not British power in the world is self-evident. If English has lost its "implication of cultural or political dominance" it remains the unwitting instrument of a linguistic imperialism. Paradoxically, England, which gave up an empire on which the sun never set, may have gained a more permanent dominion. Paradoxically also, those fervent Europeanists who promote the use of English as a *lingua franca* within the Old World, by so doing may yet have sold the pass to the New World.

CHAPTER 8—NOTES

(1) Figures kindly supplied by Mr James Platt, Secretary of the Central Bureau for Educational Visits and Exchanges, London.
(2) P. Burney, "L'apprentissage précoce des langues étrangères", in Tribune Libre, *Education Nationale*, Paris, November 1965.
(3) D. W. Brogan, "Unity and Liberty", Part 2, Section 5, in *The American Character* (Vintage Books, New York, 1959 edition), pp. 161 *et seq.*

Foreign Languages and Education in Western Europe

APPENDIX

The order of priority of foreign languages studied at the upper academic secondary level in certain countries

Country	Foreign Language						
	Eng	Fr	Ge	Ru	It	Sp	Other
Bg	2	*	3		4	5	1 (Neth)
Cy	1	2					
Dk	1	3	2	4			
Fi	2	4=	3	4=			1 (Sd)
Fr	1	*	2	5	4	3	
Ge	1	2	*	3	5	4	
Ir	*	1	3		4	2	
It	1	2	3		*	4	
Lux	3	1	2		5	4	
Ma	1	3			2		
Neth	1=	1=	1=				
Sp	2	1	3		4		
Tu	1	2	3				
UK(E)	*	1	2	4	5	3	

Notes

Bg Applies only to the French-speaking sector and to the Brussels area. In the south English is tending to have priority, with the exception of Brussels, and on the linguistic frontier, where Dutch is compulsory from the third year of the primary school. In the south Dutch is optional from the fifth grade upwards.

Cy Public schools only. Turkish schools are not included.

Fi All pupils must learn Swedish. Most of those who learn German take English as a 'voluntary' language, and vice versa. Pupils opt upon entering the terminal stage. Thus a pupil who has studied Swedish and English in the 'middle' grades will most probably take German as a 'voluntary' language later. A little Spanish and some Esperanto are also taught.

Fr There are also a few hundred pupils studying a variety of other languages, including Arabic.

Ir In 1966–67 there were also some 13,500 pupils studying Irish as an alternative language.

Lux Luxembourgeois, the spoken language, is not taught at all. All pupils in the terminal stage study French, German, and English, except that English is optional for the few pupils in the *section greco-latine*.

Neth All three languages are compulsory, and no priority is given to any one.

Sp Under 100 pupils each also study Arabic and Portuguese.